FIRST SHOLDER SHAPING

Next row: Work in pattern across each of first 18 [20, 22] sts, leaving rem sts unworked, turn. *(2 dc, 8 [9, 10] cross-sts)*

Next rows: Work in pattern until Shoulder is 1 inch long. At end of last row, fasten off.

2ND SHOULDER SHAPING

Next row: Sk next 18 [20, 20] sts on Front, **join** *(see Pattern Notes)* in next st, work in pattern across, turn. *(2 dc, 8 [9, 10] cross-sts)*

Next rows: Work in pattern until Shoulder is 1 inch long. At end of last row, fasten off.

BOTTOM EDGING

Row 1: Working in starting ch on opposite side of row 1, join with sc in first ch, sc in each ch across, turn.

Rows 2 & 3: Ch 1, sc in each st across, turn. At end of last row, fasten off.

BACK
MAKE 2.

Row 1: Ch 27 [29, 31], sc in 2nd ch from hook and in each ch across, turn. *(26 [28, 30] sc)*

Next rows: Rep rows 2 and 3 of Front for pattern until piece measures same length as Front. At end of last row, fasten off.

BOTTOM EDGING

Row 1: Working in starting ch on opposite side of row 1, join with sc in first ch, sc in each ch across, turn.

Rows 2 & 3: Ch 1, sc in each st across, turn. At end of last row, fasten off.

SLEEVE
MAKE 2.

Row 1: Ch 27 [29, 31], sc in 2nd ch from hook and in each ch across, turn. *(26 [28, 30] sc)*

Row 2: Ch 3, cross-st across, ending with dc in last st, turn. *(2 dc, 12 [13, 14] cross-sts)*

Row 3: Ch 1, 2 sc in first st, sc in each st across, ending with 2 sc in last st, turn. *(28 [30, 32] sc)*

Next rows: Rep rows 2 and 3 until there are a total of 44 [50, 56] sts.

Next rows: Work even in pattern until piece measures 6 [7, 8] inches from beg. At end of last row, fasten off.

BOTTOM EDGING

Row 1: Working in starting ch on opposite side of row 1, join with sc in first ch, sc in each ch across, turn.

Rows 2 & 3: Ch 1, sc in each st across, turn. At end of last row, fasten off.

HOOD

Row 1: Ch 61 [67, 71], sc in 2nd ch from hook and in each ch across, turn. *(60 [66, 70] sc)*

Next rows: Work in pattern until piece measures 6 [6½, 7] inches from beg. At end of last row, fasten off.

HOOD EDGING

Row 1: Working in starting ch on opposite side of row 1, join with sc in first ch, sc in each ch across, turn.

Row 2: Ch 1, sc in each st across. Fasten off.

ASSEMBLY

Sew Backs to Front shoulders.

Sew ends of rows on each side of Hood to Backs and Front as shown in photo.

BACK OPENING TRIM

Row 1: Working in ends of rows, join in first row of Bottom Edging on Back, evenly sp sc up across edge of Back, around back opening of Hood and down rem edge of Back to bottom edge, turn.

Row 2: Ch 1, sc in each st across. Fasten off.

FINISHING

Sew zipper according to manufacturer's instructions in Back opening with top of zipper at bottom edge of Back.

Measure 4½ [5, 5½] inches down from shoulder seam on both sides, place marker.

"B" is for Baby™

General Information

Many of the products used in this pattern book can be purchased from local craft, fabric and variety stores, or from the Annie's Attic Needlecraft Catalog (see Customer Service information on page 56).

Contents

Little Boy Blue

BLUE HOODIE
DESIGN BY MICHELE MAKS

SKILL LEVEL

INTERMEDIATE

FINISHED SIZES
Instructions given for size 6 months, with
   changes for 12 months and 24 months in [ ]

MATERIALS
- Red Heart LusterSheen fine (sport)
  weight yarn (4 oz/335 yds/
  113g per skein):
    1 [2, 3] skeins #0821 spa blue
- Size G/6/4mm crochet hook
  or size needed to obtain gauge
- Tapestry needle
- Sewing needle
- Sewing thread
- 18-inch zipper
- Stitch markers

2 FINE

GAUGE
20 sts= 4 inches

PATTERN NOTES
Chain-3 at beginning of row or round counts as
   first double crochet unless otherwise stated.

Join with slip stitch as indicated unless
   otherwise stated.

SPECIAL STITCH
Cross stitch (cross-st): Sk next st, dc in next st,
   working behind last st worked, dc in last sk st.

INSTRUCTIONS
HOODIE
FRONT
Row 1: Ch 55 [61, 65], sc in 2nd ch from hook
   and in each ch across, turn. *(54 [60, 64] sc)*

Row 2: **Ch 3** *(see Pattern Notes)*, **cross-st** *(see
   Special Stitch)* across, ending with dc in last st,
   turn. *(2 dc, 26 [29, 31] cross-sts)*

Row 3: Ch 1, sc in each st across, turn.

Next rows: Rep rows 2 and 3 for pattern until
   piece measures 9 [10, 11] inches from beg.

Fold 1 Sleeve in half lengthwise, place fold at shoulder seam, sew in place between markers.

Rep with rem Sleeve.

Sew side and Sleeve seams.

BOY WRAPPER
DESIGN BY ROBERTA MAIER

SKILL LEVEL

INTERMEDIATE

FINISHED SIZE
31 x 35 inches

MATERIALS
- Red Heart LusterSheen fine (sport) weight yarn (4 oz/335 yds/ 113g per skein):
    4 skeins #0821 spa blue
- Size F/5/3.75mm crochet hook or size needed to obtain gauge

GAUGE
5 sc = 1 inch; 3 cross-sts = 1 inch; 2 cross-st rows and 1 sc row = 1 inch

PATTERN NOTES
Chain-3 at beginning of row or round counts as first double crochet unless otherwise stated.

Join with slip stitch as indicated unless otherwise stated.

SPECIAL STITCH
Cross-stitch (cross-st): Sk next st, dc in next st, working behind dc just worked, dc in sk st.

INSTRUCTIONS
WRAPPER
Row 1: Ch 149, sc in 2nd ch from hook, sc in each ch across, turn. *(148 sc)*

Row 2: **Ch 3** *(see Pattern Notes)*, [**cross-st** *(see Special Stitch)* in next 2 sts] 73 times, dc in last st, turn. *(2 dc, 73 cross-sts)*

Row 3: Ch 1, sc in each st across, turn. *(148 sc)*

Rows 4–101: [Rep rows 2 and 3 alternately] 49 times. At the end of last row, **do not turn**.

BORDER
Rnd 1: Ch 1, sc in end of row 101, [2 sc in end of dc row, sc in end of sc row] across edge, working 3 sc in corner st, sc in each ch across opposite side of row 1, working 3 sc in corner st, [sc in end of sc row, 2 sc in end of next dc row] across edge, working 3 sc in corner st, sc in each st across row 101, working 2 sc in same sc as beg ch-1, **join** *(see Pattern Notes)* in beg sc.

Rnd 2: Ch 3, dc in each st around, working 3 dc in each center corner sc, join in 3rd ch of beg ch-3.

Rnd 3: [Ch 3, sl st in first ch of ch-3, sl st in each of next 2 dc] around, ending with last sl st in base of beg ch-3. Fasten off. ■

Baby Girl Layette

DESIGN BY **DONNA JONES**

SKILL LEVEL

EASY

FINISHED SIZE

Fits newborn to 3 months

MATERIALS

- Red Heart Baby Econo pompadour medium (worsted) weight yarn (6 oz/460 yds/170g per skein):
  5 skeins #1001 white
  1 skein #1722 light pink
- Sizes F/5/3.75mm and G/6/4mm crochet hooks or sizes needed to obtain gauge
- Tapestry needle
- Sewing needle
- White sewing thread
- White ¼-inch satin ribbon by Offray: 1⅔ yds
- Pearl ⅜-inch shank buttons: 3

GAUGE

Size F hook: 5 dc = 1 inch
Size G hook: 4 dc = 1 inch

PATTERN NOTES

Chain-3 at beginning of row or round counts as first double crochet unless otherwise stated.

Join with slip stitch as indicated unless otherwise stated.

SPECIAL STITCH

Shell: (2 dc, ch 2, 2 dc) in place indicated.

INSTRUCTIONS
JACKET
YOKE

Row 1: With size G hook and white, ch 46, dc in 4th ch from hook, dc in each of next 3 chs, *(dc, ch 2, dc) in next ch, dc in each of next 10 chs, rep from * twice, (dc, ch 2, dc) in next ch, dc in each of last 5 chs, turn. (*48 dc, 4 ch sps*)

Row 2: Ch 1, sc in each st across with (sc, ch 1, sc) in each ch sp, turn. (*56 sc, 4 ch sps*)

Row 3: **Ch 3** (*see Pattern Notes*), dc in each st across with (dc, ch 2, dc) in each ch sp, turn. (*64 dc, 4 ch sps*)

Rows 4–9: [Rep rows 2–3 alternately] 3 times. (*112 dc, 4 ch sps at end of last row*)

Row 10: Ch 1, [sc in each st across to next ch sp, sc in next ch sp, ch 9, sk next 28 sts (*armhole*), sc in next ch sp] twice, sc in each st across, turn. **Do not fasten off.** (*60 sc, 18 chs*)

SKIRT

Row 1: Working in sts and in chs, ch 1, sc in first st, sk next 2 sts, **shell** (see Special Stitch) in next st, sk next st, sc in next st, [sk next st or ch, shell in next st or ch, sk next st or ch, sc in next st or ch] across, **do not turn**, drop lp from hook. **Do not fasten off.** (20 sc, 19 shells)

Row 2: With RS facing, **join** (see Pattern Notes) pink in first st on row 1 of Skirt, sl st in each st and in each ch across, turn. Fasten off pink.

Row 3: Pick up dropped white lp, **ch 3** (see Pattern Notes), working over sl sts, *shell in ch sp of next shell**, dc in next sc, rep from * across, turn. Drop lp from hook.

Row 4: Join pink in first st on last row, sl st in each st and in each ch across, **do not turn**. Fasten off pink.

Row 5: Pick up dropped white lp, ch 3, working over sl sts, *shell in ch sp of next shell**, **fpdc** (see Stitch Guide) around next dc, rep from * across, ending last rep at **, dc in last st, do not turn. Drop lp from hook.

Row 6: Join pink in first st on last row, sl st in each st and in each ch across, turn. Fasten off pink.

Row 7: Pick up dropped white lp, ch 3, working over sl sts, *shell in ch sp of next shell**, **bpdc** (see Stitch Guide) around next post st, rep from * across, ending last rep at **, dc in last st, turn. Drop lp from hook.

Rows 8–22: [Rep rows 4–7 consecutively] 4 times, ending last rep with row 6. At end of last row, fasten off.

SLEEVES

Rnd 1: With size G hook, working in rem lps on opposite side of ch-9 and in sts across armhole, join white with sc in last lp of ch-9, shell in next st on armhole, [sk next st or ch, sc in next st or ch, sk next 2 sts or chs, shell in next st or ch] around **do not turn, join** (see Pattern Notes) in beg sc. Fasten off.

Rnd 2: Join pink in first sc of row 1, sl st in each st and in each ch around, join in beg sl st. Fasten off.

Rnd 3: Join white in first st, ch 3, working over sl sts, [shell in ch sp of next shell, fpdc around next sc] 6 times, shell in ch sp of next shell, join in 3rd ch of beg ch-3. Drop lp from hook.

Rnd 4: Join pink in last st, sl st in each st and ch around, join in beg sl st. Fasten off.

Rnd 5: Pick up dropped white lp, working over sl sts, ch 3, [shell in ch sp of next shell, fpdc around next dc] 6 times, shell in ch sp of next shell, join in 3rd ch of beg ch-3. Drop lp from hook.

Rnds 6–18: [Rep rows 4 and 5 alternately] 6 times, ending last rep with rnd 4. At end of last rnd, fasten off.

Rep on other armhole.

EDGING

With RS facing and size G hook, join white with sc in last sl st on row 22 of Skirt, [ch 2, sc in end of next pink row] 9 times, sk next pink row, shell in end of next sc row on Yoke, [sc in end of next dc row, shell in end of next sc row] 4 times, sc in last dc row, working in starting ch on opposite side of row 1, sc in first ch, ch 1, [sc in next ch, ch 1, sk next ch] 21 times, [sc in next ch, ch 1] twice, working in ends of rows, sc in first dc row, shell in end of next sc row, [sc in end of next dc row, shell in end of next sc row] 4 times, sk next sc row, shell in next sc row on skirt, sk next pink row, sc in end of next pink row, [ch 2, sc in end of next pink row] across. Fasten off.

Sew buttons to center of shells on left side of Jacket.

Use ch sps of shells on right side for buttonholes.

BONNET

Rnd 1: With size F hook and white, ch 3, sl st in first ch to form ring, 8 sc in ring, join in beg sc, turn. *(8 sc)*

Rnd 2: Ch 3, 2 dc in same st, 3 dc in each st around, join in 3rd ch of beg ch-3, turn. *(24 dc)*

Rnd 3: Ch 1, sc in each st around, join in beg sc, turn.

Rnd 4: Ch 3, dc in same st, 2 dc in each st around, join in 3rd ch of beg ch-3, turn. *(48 dc)*

Rnd 5: Ch 1, sc in each st around, join in beg sc, turn.

Rnd 6: Ch 3, dc in each st around, join in 3rd ch of beg ch-3, turn.

Rnd 7: Ch 1, sc in each st around, join in beg sc, turn.

Rnd 8: Ch 3, dc in same st, 2 dc in each st around, join in 3rd ch of beg ch-3, turn. *(96 dc)*

Rnds 9–14: [Rep rnds 5 and 6 alternately] 3 times.

Rnd 15: Ch 1, sc in each of first 2 sts, **sc dec** *(see Stitch Guide)* in next 2 sts, [sc in each of next 2 sts, sc dec in next 2 sts] around, join in beg sc, turn. *(72 sc)*

Rnd 16: Ch 3, dc in each of next 3 sts, dc dec in next 2 sts, [dc in each of next 4 sts, dc dec in next 2 sts] around, join in 3rd ch of beg ch-3. *(60 dc)*

Rnd 17: Ch 1, sc in each st around, join in beg sc, turn.

Rnd 18: Ch 4 *(counts as first dc and ch sp)*, [sk next st, dc in next st, ch 1] around, join in 3rd ch of beg ch-4, turn. *(30 dc, 30 ch sps)*

Rnd 19: Ch 1, sc in each st and in each ch around, join in beg sc, turn. *(60 sc)*

Rnd 20: Ch 1, sc in first st, sk next st, **shell** *(see Special Stitch)* in next st, sk next st, [sc in next st, sk next st, shell in next st, sk next st] around, join in beg sc. Fasten off.

Rnd 21: With RS facing, join pink in first st, sl st in each st and in each ch around, join in beg sl st. Fasten off.

Weave 32-inch piece of ribbon through ch sps on rnd 18, tie in 3-inch bow, trim off excess ribbon.

BOOTIE
MAKE 2.
INSTEP

Rnd 1: With size F hook and white, ch 3, 11 dc in 3rd ch from hook, join in 3rd ch of beg ch-3. *(12 dc)*

Rnd 2: Ch 1, (sc, ch 2, hdc) in first st, sc in each of next 3 sts, (hdc, 2 dc) in next st, 2 dc in each of next 7 sts, dc in same st as first sc, join in 2nd ch of beg ch-2. Fasten off. *(23 sts)*

SOLE

Rnd 1: With size F hook and white, ch 14, 2 dc in 4th ch from hook, dc in each of next 9 chs, 7 dc in next ch, working on opposite side of starting ch, dc in each of next 9 chs, 2 dc in last ch, join 3rd ch of beg ch-3. *(30 dc)*

Rnd 2: Ch 1, sc in first st, 2 sc in each of next 2 sts, sc in next st, hdc in each of next 4 sts, dc in each of next 4 sts, 2 dc in each of next 7 sts, dc in each of next 4 sts, hdc in each of next 4 sts, sc in next st, 2 sc in each of last 2 sts, join in beg sc. *(41 sts)*

Rnd 3: Ch 1, **bpsc** *(see Stitch Guide)* around each st of last rnd, join in beg sc.

SIDES

Rnd 4: Ch 3, dc in each st around, join in 3rd ch of beg ch-3.

Rnd 5: Ch 1, sc in each of first 11 sts, hold last rnd of Instep over last rnd of Sides with WS tog, working in **back lps** *(see Stitch Guide)* of both thicknesses at the same time, sl st in each of next 18 sts, leaving rem sts of Instep unworked, working through both lps of Side sts only, sc in each of last 12 sts, join in beg sc. *(18 sl sts, 23 sc)*

CUFF

Rnd 6: Ch 1, sc in each of first 11 sts, sc in each of next 5 unworked sts on Instep, sc in each of last 12 sts, join in beg sc, **do not turn.** *(28 sc)*

Rnd 7: Ch 4, sk next st, [dc in next st, ch 1, sk next st] around, join in 3rd ch of beg ch-4, turn. *(14 dc, 14 ch sps)*

Rnd 8: Ch 1, sc in each st and in each ch sp around, join in beg sc, turn.

Rnd 9: Ch 1, sc in first st, sk next st, shell in next st, [sk next 2 sts, sc in next st, sk next 2 sts, shell in next st] 4 times, sk last st, join in beg sc, do not turn. Drop lp from hook. *(5 shells, 5 sc)*

Rnd 10: Join pink in first st, sl st in each st and in each ch around, join in beg sl st, turn. Fasten off pink.

Rnd 11: Pick up dropped lp, working over sl sts, ch 3, shell in ch sp of next shell, [bpdc around next sc, shell in ch sp of next shell] around, join in 3rd ch of beg ch-3, turn. Drop lp from hook.

Rnd 12: Rep rnd 10, do not turn.

Rnd 13: Pick up dropped lp, ch 3, shell in ch sp of next shell, *fpdc *(see Stitch Guide)* around next dc, shell in ch sp of next shell, rep from * around, join in 3rd ch of beg ch-3. Fasten off.

Rnd 14: Rep rnd 10.

Beg and end at center front, weave 14-inch piece of ribbon through sts on rnd 7, tie ends in 3-inch bow.

COVERLET

Rnd 1: With size F hook and white, ch 6, sl st in first ch to form ring, ch 3, dc in ring, (ch 2, 2 dc in ring, ch 1, 2 dc in ring) 3 times, ch 2, 2 dc in ring, join with sc *(counts as ch-1)* in top of ch-3. *(16 dc, 4 ch-2 sps, 4 ch-1 sps)*

Rnd 2: Sl st in first ch-1 sp, ch 4, *(2 dc, ch 2, 2 dc) in next ch-2 sp, ch 1, dc in next ch-1 sp, ch 1, rep from * twice, (2 dc, ch 2, 2 dc) in next ch-2 sp, ch 1, join in 3rd ch of beg ch-4.

Rnd 3: Ch 3, dc in each ch-1 sp and in each st around with (2 dc, ch 2, 2 dc) in each corner ch sp, join in 3rd ch of beg ch-3.

Rnd 4: Ch 4, *sk next st, [dc in next st, ch 1, sk next st] across to next corner ch-2 sp, (2 dc, ch 2, 2 dc, ch 1) in corner ch sp, rep from * 3 times, sk next st, [dc in next st, ch 1, sk next st] across, join in 3rd ch of beg ch-4.

Rnds 5–19: [Rep rnds 3 and 4 alternately] 8 times, ending last rep with rnd 3. At end of last rnd, **do not fasten off.** *(4 ch-2 sps, 300 dc at end of last rnd)*

BORDER

Rnd 1: With RS facing, (ch 5, 2 dc) in first st, sk next st, *[dc in next st, sk next st, shell in next st, sk next st] across to next corner ch sp, 3 dc in corner ch sp, sk next st, shell in next st, sk next st, rep from * 3 times, dc in next st, sk next st, [shell in next st, sk next st, dc in next st, sk next st] across, dc in same st as ch-5, join in 3rd ch of beg ch-5. Drop lp from hook. *(76 shells, 84 dc)*

Rnd 2: Join pink in first st, sl st in each st and in each ch around, join in beg sl st, turn. Fasten off pink.

Rnd 3: Pick up dropped lp, working over sl sts, (sl st, ch 5, 2 dc) in first ch sp, [fpdc around next dc, shell in ch sp of next shell] across to next corner 3-dc group, *sk next dc, 2 dc in next sp between sts, fpdc around next dc, 2 dc in next sp between sts, shell in ch sp of next shell, [fpdc around next dc, shell in ch sp of next shell] across to next corner 3-dc group, rep from * twice, sk next dc, 2 dc in next sp between sts, fpdc around next dc, 2 dc in next sp between sts, shell in ch sp of next shell, fpdc around next dc, [shell in ch sp of next shell, fpdc around next post st] across, dc in same ch sp as beg ch-5, join in 3rd ch of beg ch-5. Drop lp from hook.

Rnd 4: Join pink in first st, sl st in each st and in each ch around, join in first sl st, **do not turn**. Fasten off pink.

Rnd 5: Pick up dropped lp, working over sl sts, (sl st, ch 5, 2 dc) in first ch sp, [fpdc around next post st, shell in ch sp of next shell] across to next 5-dc group, *fpdc around next dc, shell in next dc, fpdc around next post st, shell in next dc, fpdc around next st, shell in ch sp of next shell, [fpdc around next dc, shell in ch sp of next shell] across to next corner 5-dc group, rep from * twice, fpdc around next dc, shell in next dc, fpdc around next post st, shell in next dc, fpdc around next dc, [shell in ch sp of next shell, fpdc around next post st] across, dc in same ch sp as beg ch-5, join in 3rd ch of beg ch-5. Drop lp from hook.

Rnd 6: Rep rnd 4.

Rnd 7: Pick up dropped lp, working over sl sts, (sl st, ch 5, 2 dc) in first ch sp, [fpdc around next post st, shell in ch sp of next shell] 10 times, *2 dc in last dc of same shell, fpdc around next post st, 2 dc in first st of next shell, shell in ch sp of same shell, fpdc around next post st, shell in ch sp of next shell, [fpdc around next post st, shell in ch sp of next shell] 19 times, rep from * twice, 2 dc in last dc of same shell, fpdc around next post st, 2 dc in first st of next shell, shell in ch sp of same shell, fpdc around next post st, [shell in ch sp of next shell, fpdc around next post st] 9 times, dc in same ch sp as beg ch-5, join in 3rd ch of beg ch-5. Drop lp from hook.

Rnd 8: Rep rnd 4.

Rnd 9: Pick up dropped lp, working over sl sts, (sl st, ch 5, 2 dc) in first ch sp, [fpdc around next post st, shell in ch sp of next shell] 10 times, *fpdc around next dc, shell in next dc, fpdc around next post st, shell in next dc, fpdc around next dc, shell in ch sp of next shell, [fpdc around next post st, shell in ch sp of next shell] 20 times, rep from * twice, fpdc around next dc, shell in next dc, fpdc around next post st, shell in ch sp of next shell, fpdc around next post st, [shell in ch sp of next shell, fpdc around next post st] 9 times, dc in same ch sp as beg ch-5, join in 3rd ch of beg ch-5, do not turn. Drop lp from hook.

Rnd 10: Rep rnd 4.

Rnd 11: Pick up dropped lp, working over sl sts, (sl st, ch 5, 2 dc) in first ch sp, [fpdc around next post st, shell in ch sp of next shell] 11 times, 2 dc in next sp between sts, fpdc around next post st, 2 dc in next sp between sts, shell in ch sp of next shell, *[fpdc around next post st, shell in ch sp of next shell] 22 times, 2 dc in next sp between sts, fpdc around next post st, 2 dc in next sp between sts, shell in ch sp of next shell, rep from * twice, fpdc around next post st, [shell in ch sp of next shell, fpdc around next post st] 10 times, dc in same ch sp as beg ch-5, join in 3rd ch of beg ch-5. Drop lp from hook.

Rnd 12: Rep rnd 4.

Rnd 13: Pick up dropped lp, working over sl sts, (sl st, ch 5, 2 dc) in first ch sp, [fpdc around next post st, shell in ch sp of next shell] 11 times, *fpdc around first dc of next 2-dc group, shell in next dc, fpdc around next post st, shell in first dc of next 2-dc group, fpdc around next dc, shell in ch sp of next shell, [fpdc around next post st, shell in ch sp of next shell] 22 times, rep from * twice, fpdc around first dc of next 2-dc group, shell in next dc, fpdc around next post st, shell in first dc of next 2-dc group, fpdc around next dc, [shell in ch sp of next shell, fpdc around next post st] 11 times, dc in same ch sp as beg ch-5, join in 3rd ch of beg ch-5. Fasten off.

Rnd 14: Rep rnd 4. Fasten off all colors. ∎

Colorful Blocks
Car Seat Cover

DESIGN BY **BECKY STEVENS**

SKILL LEVEL

INTERMEDIATE

FINISHED SIZE
16 x 22 inches

MATERIALS
- Caron Simply Soft Brites medium (worsted) weight yarn (6 oz/ 315 yds/170g per skein):
  1 skein each #9606 lemonade, #9607 limelight, #9610 grape, #9608 blue mint, #9601 white
- Size G/6/4mm crochet hook or size needed to obtain gauge
- Tapestry needle

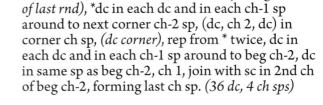

GAUGE
4 dc = 1 inch

PATTERN NOTES
Chain-2 at beginning of row or round counts as first double crochet unless otherwise stated.

Join with slip stitch as indicated unless otherwise stated.

INSTRUCTIONS
COVER
SQUARE A
MAKE 3.
Rnd 1: With lemonade, ch 4, sl st in first ch to form ring, ch 1, [sc in ring, ch 1] 8 times, **join** (see Pattern Notes) in beg sc. (8 sc)

Rnd 2: Ch 2 (see Pattern Notes), dc in same sc, ch 1, dc in next sc, ch 1, * (2 dc, ch 2, 2 dc) in next sc (corner), ch 1, dc in next sc, ch 1, rep from * twice, 2 dc in same sc as beg ch-2, ch 1, join with sc in 2nd ch of beg ch-2, forming last ch sp. (20 dc, 12 ch sps)

Rnd 3: Ch 2, dc in first st (same ch as joining sc of last rnd), *dc in each dc and in each ch-1 sp around to next corner ch-2 sp, (dc, ch 2, dc) in corner ch sp, (dc corner), rep from * twice, dc in each dc and in each ch-1 sp around to beg ch-2, dc in same sp as beg ch-2, ch 1, join with sc in 2nd ch of beg ch-2, forming last ch sp. (36 dc, 4 ch sps)

Rnd 4: Ch 2, dc in last ch sp formed, ch 1, sk beg ch-2, [dc in next dc, ch 1, sk next dc] 4 times, *(2 dc, ch 2, 2 dc) in next corner ch-2 sp (corner), ch 1, sk next dc, [dc in next dc, ch 1, sk next dc] 4 times, rep from * twice, 2 dc in same sp as beg ch-2, ch 1, join with sc in 2nd ch of beg ch-2, forming last ch sp. (32 dc, 24 ch sps)

Rnd 5: Ch 2, dc in last ch sp formed, dc in first st, *dc in each dc and ch-1 sp around to next corner ch-2 sp, (2 dc, ch 2, 2 dc) in corner ch sp, rep from * twice, dc in each dc and in each ch-1 sp around to beg ch-2, 2 dc in same ch sp as beg ch-2, ch 1, join with sc in 2nd ch of beg ch-2, **change colors** (see Stitch Guide) in last st to white. Fasten off lemonade. (4 ch sps, 68 dc)

Rnd 6: Ch 1, 2 sc in ch sp just formed, sc in first st and in each dc around to next corner ch-2 sp, (2 sc, ch 2, 2 sc) in corner ch-2 sp (corner), *sc in each dc around to next corner ch-2 sp, (2 sc, ch 2, 2 sc) in corner ch-2 sp (corner), rep from * once, sc in each dc around to next corner ch-2 sp, 2 sc in corner ch-2 sp, ch 1, join with sc in beg sc. Fasten off. (4 ch sps, 84 sc)

SQUARE B
MAKE 3.
With limelight and white, work same as Square A.

SQUARE C
MAKE 3.
With blue mint and white, work same as Square A.

SQUARE D
MAKE 3.

With grape and white, work same as Square A.

ASSEMBLY

Join Squares tog in 4 rows of 3 Squares each according to **Diagram** (see Fig 1).

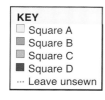

KEY
- ☐ Square A
- ☐ Square B
- ☐ Square C
- ■ Square D
- ⋯ Leave unsewn

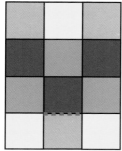

Fig. 1
Colorful Car Seat Cover
Assembly Diagram

To join Squares, hold 2 Squares with WS tog, with tapestry needle and white, sew Squares tog through **back lps** (see Stitch Guide).

Join rem Squares tog in same manner, being sure all 4-corner junctions are firmly joined.

When joining bottom 3 Squares, leave approximately 2 inches unsewn on center Squares according to Diagram to form buckle opening.

BORDER

Rnd 1 (RS): Hold piece with RS facing and 1 short end at top, join white in ch 2 sp in upper right-hand corner, ch 1, 3 sc in same sp (corner), working across side, *evenly sp [ch 1, sk next st, sc in next st] across ** to next corner, ending with ch 1, sk next st, 3 sc in corner, rep from * around, ending last rep at **, join in beg sc.

Rnd 2: Ch 1, sc first sc, 3 sc in next sc (corner), sc in each sc and in each ch-1 sp around and work 3 sc in 2nd sc of each rem corner, join in beg sc.

Rnd 3: Ch 1, sc in first 2 sc, 3 sc in next sc (corner), sc in each rem sc and work 3 sc in 2nd sc of each rem corner, join in beg sc. Fasten off. ■

Cozy Baby Bunting

DESIGN BY **ALICE HYCHE**

SKILL LEVEL

INTERMEDIATE

FINISHED SIZE
0–6 month infant

MATERIALS
- Red Heart Soft Baby light (light worsted) weight yarn (7 oz/575 yds/198g per skein): 3 skeins #7321 powder yellow
- Sizes E/4/3.5mm and G/6/4mm crochet hooks or sizes needed to obtain gauge
- Tapestry needle
- 14mm flat buttons: 8
- Pompom maker
- Stitch markers

3 LIGHT

GAUGE
Size E hook: 5 sc = 1 inch; 11 sc rows = 2 inches
Size G hook: 17 hdc = 4 inches; 7 hdc rows = 2 inches

PATTERN NOTES
Chain-2 at beginning of row or rounds counts as first half double crochet unless otherwise stated.

Use size G hook unless otherwise stated.

Join with slip stitch as indicated unless otherwise stated.

SPECIAL STITCHES
Beginning shell (beg shell): Ch 3 *(counts as first dc)*, 4 dc in same st.
Shell: 5 dc in next st.

INSTRUCTIONS
BUNTING
BODY
Row 1: Beg at neck, ch 82, hdc in 3rd ch from hook, hdc in each of next 12 chs, 2 hdc in next ch, mark last st made, hdc in each of next 11 chs, 2 hdc in next ch, mark last st made, hdc in each of next 27 chs, 2 hdc in next ch, mark last st made, hdc in each of next 11 chs, 2 hdc in next ch, mark last st made, hdc in each of last 14 chs, turn. *(85 hdc)*

Rows 2–8: Ch 2 (*see Pattern Notes*), [hdc in each st across to next marked st, remove marker, 3 hdc in next marked st, mark last st made, hdc in same st] 4 times, hdc in each st across, turn. (*169 hdc at end of last row*)

Row 9: Ch 2, hdc in each of next 24 sts, *hdc dec (*see Stitch Guide*) in next 2 marked sts, skipping 33 sts in between (*armhole*), remove markers*, hdc in each of next 49 sts, rep between *, hdc in each of last 25 sts, turn. (*101 hdc*)

Row 10: Beg shell (*see Special Stitches*), sk next st, sc in next st, [sk next 2 sts, **shell** (*see Special Stitches*) in next st, sk next 2 sts, sc in next st] 15 times, [sk next st, shell in next st, sk next st, sc in next st] twice, turn. (*18 shells, 18 sc*)

Rows 11–45: Beg shell, sc in 3rd dc of next shell, [shell in next sc, sc in 3rd dc of next shell] across, turn. At end of last row, fasten off.

BUTTON PLACKET
Row 1: Working in ends of rows across left side, with size E hook, join with sc in first row on neck edge, evenly sp 99 sc across, turn. (*100 sc*)

Rows 2–8: Ch 1, sc in each st across, turn. At end of last row, fasten off.

BUTTONHOLE PLACKET
Row 1: Working in ends of rows across right side, with size E hook, join with sc in first row on neck edge, evenly sp 99 sc across, turn. (*100 sc*)

Rows 2–4: Ch 1, sc in each st across, turn.

Row 5: Ch 1, sc in each of first 2 sts, [ch 2, sk next 2 sts, sc in each of next 7 sts] 8 times (*buttonholes*), sc in each st across, turn. (*8 buttonholes*)

Row 6: Ch 1, sc in each st and in each ch across, turn.

Rows 7 & 8: Repeat row 2. At end of last row, fasten off.

Overlap Buttonhole Placket over Button Placket.

Sew last 5 inches of last row on Buttonhole Placket to Button Placket.

Working across rows horizontally 5 inches from bottom, sew Plackets tog.

Sew buttons to row 4 of Button Placket opposite buttonholes.

NECK EDGE
Row 1: Working in ends of rows on Plackets and in starting ch on opposite side of row 1 on neck edge, join with sc in first row, sc in each of next 6 rows, sk end of next row and next ch, sc in each ch across to last ch, sk last ch and end of next row, sc in each of last 7 rows, turn. (*93 sc*)

Row 2: Ch 1, sc in each of first 9 sts, **sc dec** (*see Stitch Guide*) in next 2 sts, [sc in each of next 2 sts, sc dec in next 2 sts] across to last 10 sts, sc in each of last 10 sts, turn. (*74 sc*)

Row 3: Ch 1, sc in each st across, turn.

Row 4: Ch 2, hdc in each st across, turn. Fasten off.

HOOD
Row 1: Sk first 11 sts on last row of Neck Edge, **join** (*see Pattern Notes*) in next st, beg shell, sk next 2 sts, sc in next st, [sk next 2 sts, shell in next st, sk next 2 sts, sc in next st] 8 times leaving rem sts unworked, turn. (*9 shells, 9 sc*)

Rows 2–13: Beg shell, sc in 3rd dc of next shell, [shell in next sc, sc in 3rd dc of next shell] across, turn. At end of last row, fasten off.

Fold last row of Hood in half, matching sts, ch 1, sc in each st across, ch 10 (*tie for Pompom*). Fasten off.

BORDER
Row 1: Working in ends of rows across Hood, join with sc in first row, evenly sp 57 sc across, turn. (*58 sc*)

Row 2: Working this row in **back lps** (*see Stitch Guide*), ch 1, sc in each st across, turn.

Row 3: Beg shell, sk next 2 sts, sc in next st, [sk next 2 sts, shell in next st, sk next 2 sts, sc in next st] across, turn. (*10 shells, 10 sc*)

Row 4: Beg shell, sc in 3rd dc of next shell, [shell in next sc, sc in 3rd dc of next shell] across, turn.

Row 5: Ch 1, sc in each st across. Fasten off.

TIE
Ch 90. Fasten off.

Starting with 2nd st on first row of Hood, weave under next shell and over next st across to last shell on Hood, weave through corner on Cuff, weave under last shell. Pull to gather, pull ends even.

POMPOM
MAKE 3.
Using pompom maker, make 2-inch pompom.

Tie 1 Pompom to end of ch on Hood and 1 Pompom to each end of Tie around neck.

BOTTOM
Rnd 1: Ch 32, sc in 2nd ch from hook, sc in each ch across with 3 sc in last ch, working on opposite side of ch, sc in each ch across with 2 sc in last ch, join in beg sc, **turn.** *(64 sc)*

Rnd 2: Ch 1, sc in first st, 3 sc in next st, sc in each st around with 3 sc in 2nd sc of next 3-sc group, join in beg sc, turn. *(68 sc)*

Rnds 3–9: Ch 1, sc in each st around with 3 sc in 2nd sc of each 3-sc group, turn. *(96 sc at end of last rnd)*

Rnd 10: Beg shell, sk next 2 sts, sc in next st, sk next 2 sts, [shell in next st, sk next 2 sts, sc in next st, sk next 2 sts] around, join in 3rd ch of beg ch-3, turn. *(16 shells, 16 sc)*

Rnd 11: Sl st in first sc, beg shell in same st, sc in 3rd dc of next shell, [shell in next sc, sc in 3rd dc of next shell] around, join in 3rd ch of beg ch-3, **do not turn.**

Rnd 12: Matching shells, working through both thicknesses and easing to fit, ch 1, sc last rnd of Bottom to bottom edge of Body, join in beg sc. Fasten off.

SLEEVES
Rnd 1: Working in sk sts on armhole of Body, join with sc in st at underarm, sc in each of next 9 sts, 2 sc in next st, [sc in each of next 10 sts, 2 sc in next st] twice, join in beg sc, turn. *(36 sc)*

Rnd 2: Rep rnd 10 of Bottom. *(6 shells, 6 sc)*

Rnds 3–14: Sl st in first sc, beg shell in same st, sc in 3rd dc of next shell, [shell in next sc, sc in 3rd dc of next shell] across, join in 3rd ch of beg ch-3, turn.

Rnd 15: Ch 1, sc in each st around, join in beg sc, turn. *(36 sc)*

Rnd 16: Ch 1, sc in first st, *[sc dec in next 2 sts] twice, sc in next st, rep from * around, join in beg sc, turn. **Do not fasten off.** *(22 sc)*

CUFF
Row 1: With size E hook, ch 13, sc in 2nd ch from hook, sc in each ch across, sl st in each of first 2 sts of Sleeve, turn. *(12 sc)*

Row 2: Working the following rows in back lps, ch 1, sc in each st across, turn.

Row 3: Ch 1, sc in each st across, sl st in each of next 2 sts of Sleeve, turn.

Rows 4–22: [Rep rows 2 and 3 alternately] 10 times, ending last rep with row 2. At end of last row, leaving long end, fasten off.

Using long end, sew back lps of first and last rows tog.

Fold Cuff back.

Rep Sleeve in opposite armhole. ∎

Pink & Blue Bears

DESIGN BY **SHEILA LESILE**

SKILL LEVEL

INTERMEDIATE

FINISHED SIZE

12½ inches tall in sitting position

MATERIALS

- TLC Baby Amoré medium (worsted) weight yarn (5 oz/ 279 yds/140g per skein):
  2 skeins each #9781 rose or #9832 light blue
  ¼ oz/12 yds/7g black
- Size K/10½/6.5mm crochet hook or size needed to obtain gauge
- Tapestry needle
- Fiberfill
- 15mm black shank buttons: 2
- 1-inch-wide ribbon: 1 yd
- Stitch marker

GAUGE

2 strands held tog: 3 sc = 1 inch

PATTERN NOTES

If being made for a toy, work satin stitch for eyes instead of using buttons which may be swallowed by a child.

Hold 2 strands together throughout unless otherwise stated.

Work in continuous rounds, do not turn or join unless otherwise stated.

Place marker in first stitch of round.

Join with slip stitch as indicated unless otherwise stated.

INSTRUCTIONS

BEAR

HEAD

Rnd 1: Beg at muzzle, with **2 strands held tog** (*see Pattern Notes*), ch 2, 6 sc in 2nd ch from hook, **do not join** (*see Pattern Notes*). (*6 sc*)

Rnd 2: [Sc in next st, 2 sc in next st] around. (*9 sc*)

Rnds 3 & 4: [Sc in each of next 2 sts, 2 sc in next st] around. (*16 sc at end of last rnd*)

Rnd 5: [2 sc in next st, sc in each of next 3 sts] around. *(20 sc)*

Rnd 6: Sc in each st around.

Rnd 7: Sc in each of first 8 sts, 2 sc in each of next 4 sts, sc in each of last 8 sts. *(24 sc)*

Rnd 8: Sc in each of first 8 sts, [sc in next st, 2 sc in next st] 4 times, sc in each of last 8 sts, *(28 sc)*

Rnd 9: [Sc in each of next 3 sts, 2 sc in next st] around. *(35 sc)*

Rnd 10: [Sc in each of next 6 sts, 2 sc in next st] around. *(40 sc)*

Rnds 11–17: Sc in each st around.

Rnd 18: [Sc in each of next 8 sts, **sc dec** *(see Stitch Guide)* in next 2 sts] around. *(36 sc)*

Rnd 19: [Sc in each of next 4 sts, sc dec in next 2 sts] around. Stuff Head. *(30 sc)*

Rnd 20: [Sc in each of next 3 sts, sc dec in next 2 sts] around. *(24 sc)*

Rnd 21: [Sc in each of next 2 sts, sc dec in next 2 sts] around. *(18 sc)*

Rnd 22: [Sc in next st, sc dec in next 2 sts] around. Finish stuffing Head. *(12 sc)*

Rnd 23: [Sc dec in next 2 sts] around, **join** *(see Pattern Notes)* in beg sc. Leaving long end, fasten off.

Weave long end through sts of last rnd, pull to close. Secure end.

FINISHING

Sew buttons to Head above muzzle 1 inch apart for eyes or work **satin stitch** *(see Pattern Notes)*.

Using **satin stitch** *(see Fig. 1)*, with black, embroider nose on muzzle as shown in photo.

Fig. 1
Satin Stitch

Using **straight stitch** *(see Fig. 2)*, with black, embroider mouth across end of muzzle below nose as shown in photo.

Fig. 2
Straight Stitch

EAR
MAKE 2.

Row 1: Ch 2, 6 sc in 2nd ch from hook, turn. *(6 sc)*

Row 2: Ch 1, sc in first st, 2 hdc in next st, 2 dc in each of next 2 sts, 2 hdc in next st, sc in next st, turn. *(10 sts)*

Row 3: Ch 1, sc in each of first 3 sts, 2 sc in each of next 4 sts, sc in each of last 3 sts. Fasten off.

Sew Ears to Head 2½ inches apart as shown in photo.

BODY

Rnd 1: Ch 24, sc in first ch to form ring, sc in each ch around, **do not join**. *(24 sc)*

Rnd 2: [Sc in each of next 3 sts, 2 sc in next st] around. *(30 sc)*

Rnd 3: Sc in each st around.

Rnd 4: [Sc in each of next 4 sts, 2 sc in next st] around. *(36 sc)*

Rnd 5: Sc in each st around.

Rnd 6: [Sc in each of next 8 sts, 2 sc in next st] around. *(40 sc)*

Rnd 7: Sc in each st around.

Rnd 8: [Sc in each of next 9 sts, 2 sc in next st] around. *(44 sc)*

Rnd 9: Sc in each st around.

Rnd 10: [Sc in each of next 10 sts, 2 sc in next st] around. Stuff Body. *(48 sc)*

Rnds 11–19: Sc in each st around.

Rnd 20: [Sc in each of next 6 sts, sc dec in next 2 sts] around. *(42 sc)*

Rnd 21: [Sc in each of next 5 sts, sc dec in next 2 sts] around. *(36 sc)*

Rnd 22: [Sc in each of next 4 sts, sc dec in next 2 sts] around. *(30 sc)*

Rnd 23: [Sc in each of next 3 sts, sc dec in next 2 sts] around. *(24 sc)*

Rnd 24: [Sc in each of next 2 sts, sc dec in next 2 sts] around. *(18 sc)*

Rnd 25: [Sc in next st, sc dec in next 2 sts] around. Finish stuffing Body. *(12 sc)*

Rnd 26: [Sc dec in next 2 sts] around, join in beg sc. Leaving long end, fasten off.

Weave long end through sts on last rnd, pull to close. Secure end.

Sew Head to Body.

LEG
MAKE 2.

Rnd 1: Ch 2, 6 sc in 2nd ch from hook, **do not join**. *(6 sc)*

Rnd 2: 2 sc in each st around. *(12 sc)*

Rnd 3: [Sc in next st, 2 sc in next st] around. *(18 sc)*

Rnd 4: [Sc in each of next 2 sts, 2 sc in next st] around. *(24 sc)*

Rnds 5–15: Sc in each st around. At end of last rnd, join in beg sc. Fasten off.

Stuff.

Sew Legs to Body in sitting position as shown in photo.

ARM
MAKE 2.

Rnd 1: Ch 2, 6 sc in 2nd ch from hook, **do not join**. *(6 sc)*

Rnd 2: 2 sc in each st around. *(12 sc)*

Rnd 3: [Sc in next st, 2 sc in next st] around. *(18 sc)*

Rnds 4–15: Sc in each st around. At end of last rnd, join in beg sc. Fasten off.

Stuff.

Sew Arms to Body above Legs as shown in photo.

Tie ribbon in bow around neck. Trim ends. ■

Bear Security Blankie

DESIGN BY **ASHLEY IVEY**

SKILL LEVEL

INTERMEDIATE

FINISHED SIZE
14 inches square

MATERIALS
- Red Heart Super Saver medium (worsted) weight yarn (7 oz/ 364 yds/198g per skein):
    1 skein each #316 soft white and #381 light blue
    1 yd #312 black
- Size J/10/6mm crochet hook or size needed to obtain gauge
- Tapestry needle

4 MEDIUM

GAUGE
2 dc and 1 sc rows = 1½ inches

PATTERN NOTES
Chain-3 at beginning of row or round counts as first double crochet unless otherwise stated.

Join with slip stitch as indicated unless otherwise stated.

When changing colors, always change in last stitch worked.

Chain-4 at beginning of row or round counts as first treble crochet unless otherwise stated.

SPECIAL STITCH
Cluster (cl): Holding back last lp of each st on hook, 3 dc in place indicated, yo, pull through all lps on hook.

INSTRUCTIONS
BLANKIE

Rnd 1: Ch 3, sl st in first ch to form ring, ch 1, 8 sc in ring, **join** (*see Pattern Notes*) in beg sc. (*8 sc*)

Rnd 2: Ch 3 (*see Pattern Notes*), dc in same st, 2 dc in each st around, join in 3rd ch of beg ch-3. (*16 dc*)

Rnd 3: Ch 1, sc in first st, ch 3, sk next st, [sc in next st, ch 3, sk next st] around, join in beg sc. (*8 ch sps*)

Rnd 4: Sl st in first ch sp, ch 3, 3 dc in same ch sp, 4 dc in each ch sp around, join in 3rd ch of beg ch-3. (*32 dc*)

Rnd 5: Ch 1, sc in first st, ch 3, sk next st, [sc in next st, ch 3, sk next st] around, join in beg sc. (*16 ch sps*)

Rnd 6: Sl st in first ch sp, ch 3, 3 dc in same ch sp, 4 dc in each ch sp around, **changing colors** (*see Stitch Guide and Pattern Notes*) to light blue, join in 3rd ch of beg ch-3. **Do not fasten off soft white.** (*64 dc*)

Rnd 7: With light blue, ch 1, sc in first st, ch 3, sk next st, [sc in next st, ch 3, sk next st] around, changing to soft white, join in beg sc. Fasten off light blue. (*32 ch sps*)

Rnd 8: With soft white, sl st in first ch sp, **ch 4** (*see Pattern Notes*), (tr, ch 2, 2 tr) in same ch sp (*corner*), *2 dc in next ch sp, 2 hdc in next ch sp, 2 sc in each of next 3 ch sps, 2 hdc in next ch sp, 2 dc in next ch sp**, (2 tr, ch 2, 2 tr) in next ch sp (*corner*), rep from * around, ending last rep at **, join in 4th ch of beg ch-4.

Rnd 9: Sl st in next st and next ch sp, ch 3, (2 dc, ch 2, 3 dc) in same ch sp, *dc in each st across to corner ch sp**, (3 dc, ch 3, 3 dc) in next corner ch sp, rep from * around, ending last rep at **, changing to light blue in last st, join in 3rd ch of beg ch-3.

Rnd 10: Ch 1, sc in first st and in each st around with 3 sc in each corner ch sp, changing to soft white, join in beg sc. Fasten off light blue.

Rnd 11: With soft white, ch 3, *dc in each st across to center corner st**, (3 dc, ch 3, 3 dc) in next corner st, rep from * around, ending last rep at **, join in 3rd ch of beg ch-3.

Rnd 12: Ch 3, dc in each st around with (3 dc, ch 2, 3 dc) in each corner ch sp, join in 3rd ch of beg ch-3. Fasten off.

Rnd 13: Join light blue in any corner ch sp, ch 3, (2 dc, ch 3, 3 dc) in same ch sp, *sk next 2 sts, [5 dc in next st, sk next 3 sts] across to corner ch sp**, (3 dc, ch 3, 3 dc) in next corner ch sp, rep from * around, ending last rep at **, join in 3rd ch of beg ch-3. Fasten off.

Rnd 14: Join soft white with sc in any corner ch sp, 4 sc in same ch sp, sc in each st around with 5 sc in each corner ch sp, join in beg sc. Fasten off.

BEAR
HEAD
FACE

Rnd 1: Beg at muzzle, ch 4, sl st in first ch to form ring, ch 3, 11 dc in ring, join in 3rd ch of beg ch-3. Fasten off. (*12 dc*)

Rnd 2: Join light blue with sc in first st, sc in each st around, join in beg sc.

Rnd 3: Ch 3, dc in same st, 2 dc in each of next 6 sts, 2 hdc in each of last 5 sts, join in 3rd ch of beg ch-3. (*24 sts*)

Rnd 4: Ch 1, sc in first st, hdc in next st, 2 dc in each of next 3 sts, 2 tr in each of next 4 sts, 2 dc in each of next 4 sts, hdc in next st, sc in each st around, join in beg sc. Leaving long end, fasten off.

EARS

Beg with first st after joining on rnd 4, count over 8 sts, join light blue with sc in 8th st, (hdc, dc, hdc, sc) in same st, sl st in next 7 sts, (sc, hdc, dc, hdc, sc) in next st. Fasten off.

FINISHING

Using **French knot** (*see Fig. 1*), with black, embroider 2 eyes on Face as shown in photo.

Fig. 1
French Knot

With black, leaving long end, ch 3, **cl** (*see Special Stitch*) in 3rd ch from hook. Leaving long end, fasten off.

Fold in half and sew securely to center of Face for nose as shown in photo.

BACK

Rnd 1: With light blue, ch 3, sl st in first ch to form ring, ch 1, 9 sc in ring, join in beg sc. (*9 sc*)

Rnd 2: Ch 3, dc in same st, 2 dc in each st around, join in 3rd ch of beg ch-3. (*18 dc*)

Rnd 3: Ch 3, dc in same st, 2 dc in each st around, join in 3rd ch of beg ch-3. **Do not fasten off.** (*36 dc*)

EARS

Ch 1, (sc, hdc, dc, hdc, sc) in next st, sl st in each of next 7 sts, (sc, hdc, dc, hdc, sc) in next st. Fasten off.

ARMS

Row 1: With light blue, ch 28, sc 2nd ch from hook and in each ch across, turn. (*27 sc*)

Row 2: Ch 2 (*counts as first hdc*), hdc in each st across.

Row 3: Working through both thicknesses, count 13 sts from center of 1 corner on Blanket, ch 1, sc in each st across corner and other edge. Fasten off.

Sew Face and Back WS over Arms at corner as shown in photo. ■

Tiny Teddies Mobile

DESIGN BY **SHEILA LESLIE**

SKILL LEVEL

EASY

FINISHED SIZE

Bear: 5½ inches tall

MATERIALS

- Bernat Softee Baby light (light worsted) weight yarn (5 oz/ 468 yds/140g per skein): 1 oz/100 yds/28g each #02000 white, #02001 pink, #02003 lemon, #02002 pale blue and #02004 mint
- Medium (worsted) weight yarn: 2 yds black
- Size G/6/4mm crochet hook or size needed to obtain gauge
- Tapestry needle
- Fiberfill
- 9-inch metal ring
- 1½-inch plastic ring
- Stitch marker

GAUGE

5 sc = 1 inch

PATTERN NOTES

Work in continuous rounds, do not join or turn unless otherwise stated.

Mark first stitch of each round.

Join with slip stitch as indicated unless otherwise stated.

For safety's sake, hang out of reach of baby.

INSTRUCTIONS

BEAR

MAKE 1 EACH WITH PINK, PALE BLUE, LEMON AND MINT.

HEAD

Rnd 1: Beg at top of Head with color, ch 2, 6 sc in 2nd ch from hook, **do not join** (see Pattern Notes). (6 sc)

Rnd 2: 2 sc in each sc around. (12 sc)

Rnd 3: [Sc in next sc, 2 sc in next sc] around. (18 sc)

Rnd 4: [2 sc in next sc, sc in each of next 2 sc] around. (24 sc)

Rnd 5: Sc in each sc around.

Rnd 6: [Sc in each of next 7 sc, 2 sc in next sc] around. (27 sc)

Rnds 7–12: Rep rnd 5.

Rnd 13: [Sc in next sc, **sc dec** (*see Stitch Guide*) in next 2 sc] around. Stuff Head with fiberfill. (*18 sc*)

Rnd 14: [Sc dec in next 2 sc] 9 times. (*9 sc*)

BODY

Rnd 15: Rep rnd 2. (*18 sc*)

Rnd 16: [Sc in each of next 2 sc, 2 sc in next sc] around. (*24 sc*)

Rnd 17: [2 sc in next sc, sc in each of next 3 sc] around. (*30 sc*)

Rnds 18–27: Rep rnd 5.

Rnd 28: [Sc in each of next 3 sc, sc dec in next 2 sc] around. Stuff Body with fiberfill. (*24 sc*)

Rnd 29: [Sc in next sc, sc dec in next 2 sc] around. (*16 sc*)

Rnd 30: [Sc dec in next 2 sc] around. (*8 sc*)

Rnd 31: Rep rnd 30, **join** (*see Pattern Notes*) in beg sc. Fasten off. (*4 sc*)

SNOUT

Rnd 1: With white, ch 2, 4 sc in 2nd ch from hook, **do not join**. (*4 sc*)

Rnd 2: 2 sc in each sc around. (*8 sc*)

Rnd 3: [2 sc in each of next 2 sc, sc in each of next 2 sc] around. (*12 sc*)

Rnd 4: Sc in each sc around, join in beg sc. Fasten off.

Sew Snout to front of Head as shown in photo, stuffing with fiberfill before closing.

EAR
MAKE 2.

Row 1: With color, ch 2, 4 sc in 2nd ch from hook, turn. (*4 sc*)

Row 2: Ch 1, sc in first sc, 2 sc in each of next 2 sc, (sc, sl st) in last sc. Fasten off.

Sew Ears to Head as shown in photo.

LEG
MAKE 2.

Rnd 1: Beg at bottom of Leg, with white, ch 2, 6 sc in 2nd ch from hook, **do not join**. (*6 sc*)

Rnd 2: 2 sc in each sc around. (*12 sc*)

Rnd 3: [Sc in each of next 3 sc, 2 sc in next sc] 3 times, join in beg sc. Fasten off. (*15 sc*)

Rnd 4: Working in **back lps** (*see Stitch Guide*) of sts, join color with sc in first st, sc in each st around.

Rnds 5–8: Sc in each sc around.

Rnd 9: [Sc in each of next 4 sc, 2 sc in next sc] 3 times. (*18 sc*)

Rnd 10: Sc in each sc around, join in beg sc. Fasten off.

Stuff Legs with fiberfill and sew to bottom of Body as shown in photo.

ARM
MAKE 2.

Rnd 1: Beg at bottom of Arm with white, ch 2, 6 sc in 2nd ch from hook, do not join. (*6 sc*)

Rnd 2: 2 sc in each sc around. (*12 sc*)

Rnd 3: [Sc in each of next 5 sc, 2 sc in next sc] twice, join in beg sc. Fasten off. (*14 sc*)

Rnds 4–8: Rep rnds 4–8 of Leg.

Rnd 9: Sc in each sc around, join in beg sc. Fasten off.

Stuff Arms with fiberfill and sew an Arm to each side of Body as shown in photo.

FACIAL FEATURES

Using **satin stitch** *(see Fig. 1)*, with black, embroider eyes above snout and nose as shown in photo.

Fig. 1
Satin Stitch

Using **straight stitches** *(see Fig. 2)* with black, embroider nose and mouth lines centered on Snout as shown in photo.

Fig. 2
Straight Stitch

HANGER
METAL RING

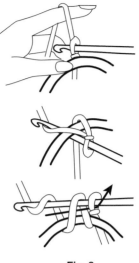

Fig. 3
Single Crochet Around Ring

Rnd 1: Work 24 sc around metal ring *(see Fig. 3)* with each color in the following color sequence: white, pale blue, white, lemon, white, mint, white and pink. Carry white along as work progresses and drop rem colors to WS as work progresses, join in beg sc. *(192 sc)*

Rnd 2: Maintaining the same color sequence as previous rnd 1, ch 1, sc in same sc as beg ch-1, [sk next sc, 5 dc in next sc, sk next sc, sc in next sc] 5 times, sk next sc, 5 dc in next sc, **change color** *(see Stitch Guide)* to next color in sequence and carry white along, working over as work progresses and finish off colored yarn at end of each section, with color, *[sk next sc, sc in next sc, sk next sc, 5 dc in next sc] 6 times, change to next color in last step of 5th dc, rep from * around, sk last st, join in beg sc. Fasten off.

PLASTIC RING

Join white to Plastic Ring, ch 1, 32 sc around Plastic Ring *(see Fig. 3)*, join in beg sc. Fasten off.

HANGING CHAIN
MAKE 4.

With white, ch 36. Fasten off.

Sew first end to center of white section of rnd 2 on Metal Ring, sew opposite end to sc on Plastic Ring. Rep with rem chs attaching evenly sp to Metal and Plastic Rings.

BEAR CHAIN
MAKE 4.

With color of each Bear, ch 24. Fasten off.

Sew first end of ch to center top of Head and opposite end to rnd 2 of Metal Ring, centered on same color section as Bear. ■

Bear
Blanket

DESIGN BY **MICHELE MAKS**

SKILL LEVEL

INTERMEDIATE

FINISHED SIZE
45 inches square, excluding edging

MATERIALS
- Red Heart Super Saver medium (worsted) weight yarn (7 oz/ 364 yds/198g per skein):
  - 3 skeins #316 soft white
  - 1 skein each #722 pretty 'n pink, #381 light blue, #672 spring green and #324 bright yellow
- Size J/10/6mm crochet hook or size needed to obtain gauge
- Tapestry needle

GAUGE
5 sc = 1¾ inches; 5 sc rows = 1¾ inches

PATTERN NOTE
Join with slip stitch as indicated unless otherwise stated.

INSTRUCTIONS
BLANKET
SQUARE
MAKE 13 SOFT WHITE, 3 EACH PRETTY 'N PINK, LIGHT BLUE, SPRING GREEN AND BRIGHT YELLOW.
Row 1: Ch 27, sc in 2nd ch from hook and in each ch across, turn. *(26 sc)*

Rows 2–26: Ch 1, sc in each st across, turn. At end of last row, fasten off.

FINISHING

Using **cross-stitch** (*see Fig. 1*), with soft white, embroider Bear according to chart (*see Fig. 2*) on each pretty 'n pink, light blue, spring green and bright yellow Square.

Fig. 1
Cross-Stitch

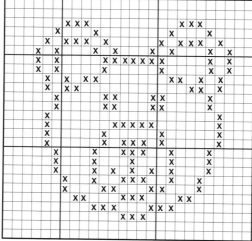

Fig. 2
Chart

Sew Squares WS tog according to Assembly Diagram (*see Fig. 3*).

EDGING

Rnd 1: With WS facing, join soft white with sc in first st at top right-hand corner, 2 sc in same st, evenly sp sc across with 3 sc in last st, working in ends of rows, evenly sp sc across, working in starting ch on opposite side of row 1, 3 sc in first ch, sc in each ch across with 3 sc in last ch, working in ends of rows, evenly sp sc across, **join** (*see Pattern Note*) in beg sc, **turn**.

Rnds 2–4: Ch 1, sc in each st around with 3 sc in each center corner st, join in beg sc. At end of last row, fasten off. ■

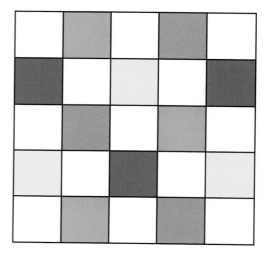

Fig. 3
Bear Blanket
Assembly Diagram

FROG Baby Bib

DESIGN BY **SHEILA LESLIE**

SKILL LEVEL

INTERMEDIATE

FINISHED SIZE
One size fits most

MATERIALS
- Medium (worsted) weight cotton yarn:
  1¾ oz/88 yds/50g bright green
  ¼ oz/13 yds/7g each black and white
- Size H/8/5mm crochet hook or size needed to obtain gauge
- Tapestry needle
- Sewing needle
- Sewing thread
- 5-inch strip hook-and-loop fastener

GAUGE
4 sc = 1 inch

PATTERN NOTES
Chain-3 at beginning of row or round counts as first double crochet unless otherwise stated.

Join with slip stitch as indicated unless otherwise stated.

INSTRUCTIONS
BIB
Rnd 1: With bright green, ch 4, sl st in first ch to form ring, **ch 3** (see Pattern Notes), 11 dc in ring, **join** (see Pattern Notes) in 3rd ch of beg ch-3. (12 dc)

Rnd 2: Ch 3, dc in same st, 2 dc in each st around, join in 3rd ch of beg ch-3. (24 dc)

Rnd 3: Ch 3, 2 dc in next st, [dc in next st, 2 dc in next st] around, join in 3rd ch of beg ch-3. (36 dc)

Rnd 4: Ch 3, dc in next st, 2 dc in next st, [dc in each of next 2 sts, 2 dc in next st] around, join in 3rd ch of beg ch-3. (48 dc)

Rnd 5: Ch 3, dc in each of next 2 sts, 2 dc in next st, [dc in each of next 3 sts, 2 dc in next st] around, join in 3rd ch of beg ch-3. (60 dc)

Rnd 6: Ch 3, dc in each of next 3 sts, 2 dc in next st, [dc in each of next 4 sts, 2 dc in next st,] around, join in 3rd ch of beg ch-3. (72 dc)

Rnd 7: Ch 3, dc in each of next 4 sts, 2 dc in next st, [dc in each of next 5 sts, 2 dc in next st] around, join in 3rd ch of beg ch-3. (84 dc)

FIRST STRAP
Row 8: Now working in rows, ch 1, hdc in first st and in each of next 7 sts, leaving rem sts unworked, turn. (8 sc)

Row 9: Ch 1, 2 hdc in first st, hdc in each st across with **hdc dec** (see Stitch Guide) in last 2 sts, turn.

Row 10: Ch 1, hdc dec in first 2 sts, hdc in each st across with 2 hdc in last st, turn.

Rows 11–26: [Rep rows 9 and 10 alternately] 8 times. At end of last row, fasten off.

2ND STRAP
Row 8: Sk next 9 sts after last st of row 8 on First Strap, join in next st, ch 1, hdc in same st, hdc in each of next 7 sts, leaving rem sts unworked, turn. (8 hdc)

Row 9: Ch 1, hdc dec in first 2 sts, hdc in each st across with 2 hdc in last st, turn.

Row 10: Ch 1, 2 hdc in first st, hdc in each st across with hdc dec in last 2 sts, turn.

Rows 11–26: [Rep rows 9 and 10 alternately] 8 times. At end of last row, fasten off.

EYE
MAKE 2.
Rnd 1: With black, ch 4, sl st in first ch to form ring, ch 3, 11 dc in ring, join in 3rd ch of beg ch-3. Fasten off.

Rnd 2: Join white in first st, ch 3, dc in same st, 2 dc in each st around, join in 3rd ch of beg ch-3.

Rnd 3: Ch 1, sc in first st, 2 sc in next st, [sc in next st, 2 sc in next st] around, join in beg sc. Fasten off.

Rnd 4: Working in **front lps** (*see Stitch Guide*), join green in any st, sl st in each st around, join in beg sl st. Fasten off.

FINISHING
Sew Eyes to Bib below Straps as shown in photo.

Using **straight stitch** (*see Fig. 1*), with black, embroider mouth as shown in photo.

Fig. 1
Straight Stitch

Sew hook-and-loop fastener to WS of Straps. ∎

Duck
Booties & Bib

DESIGN BY **YVONNE HEALY**

SKILL LEVEL

INTERMEDIATE

FINISHED SIZES

Bootie sole: 3½ inches
Duck bib: 5½ inches in diameter

MATERIALS

- Pisgah Yarn & Dyeing Co. Inc. Peaches & Crème medium (worsted) weight cotton yarn (2 oz/98 yds/ 57g per ball):
  1 ball each #12 gold, #11 sunburst and #121 chocolate
- Sizes F/5/3.75mm and G/6/4mm crochet hooks or sizes needed to obtain gauge
- Tapestry needle

MEDIUM

GAUGE

Size F hook: 4 sc = 1 inch
Size G hook: 2 dc rnds = 1¼ inches

PATTERN NOTES

Join with slip stitch as indicated unless otherwise stated.

Chain-3 at beginning of row or round counts as first double crochet unless otherwise stated.

INSTRUCTIONS
BOOTIE
MAKE 2.
SOLE

Row 1: Beg at toe, with size F hook and gold, ch 4, sc in 2nd ch from hook and in each of next 2 chs, turn. *(3 sc)*

Row 2: Ch 1, sc in each sc across, turn.

Rows 3 & 4: Rep row 2.

Row 5: Ch 1, 2 sc in first sc, sc in next sc, 2 sc in last sc, turn. *(5 sc)*

Rows 6–10: Rep row 2.

Row 11: Rep row 2, **do not turn**.

Rnd 12: Now working in rnds and in ends of rows, ch 1, evenly sp 11 sc across side edge, 3 sc across opposite side of row 1, working in ends of rows, evenly sp 11 sc across side edge, sc in each st across row 11, **join** *(see Pattern Notes)* in beg sc. *(30 sc)*

Rnd 13: Ch 1, working in **back lps** *(see Stitch Guide)*, sc in each st around, join in beg sc.

Rnd 14: Ch 1, sc in each of first 10 sc, [**sc dec** *(see Stitch Guide)* in next 2 sc] 5 times, sc in each of last 10 sc, join in beg sc. *(25 sc)*

Rnd 15: Ch 1, sc in each of first 8 sc, [sc dec in next 2 sc] 5 times, sc in each of last 7 sc, join in beg sc. *(20 sc)*

Rnd 16: Ch 1, working in back lps, sc in each st around, join in beg sc.

Rnd 17: Ch 1, sc in each of first 7 sc, [sc dec in next 2 sc] 3 times, sc in each of last 7 sc, join in beg sc. Fasten off. *(17 sc)*

Rnd 18: Join sunburst with sc at back of Bootie, sc in each sc around, join in beg sc. *(17 sc)*

Rnds 19–22: Ch 1, sc in each sc around, join in beg sc. At the end of last rnd, fasten off.

BEAK
Row 1: With size F hook and sunburst, ch 4, sc in 2nd ch from hook and in each of next 2 chs, turn. *(3 sc)*

Row 2: Ch 1, 2 sc in first sc, sc in next sc, 2 sc in last sc, turn. *(5 sc)*

Row 3: Ch 1, sc in first st, hdc in next sc, tr in next sc, hdc in next sc, sc in last sc. Fasten off.

FINISHING
Using **satin stitch** *(see Fig. 1)*, with chocolate, embroider eyes over rnd 17 at center front of Bootie as shown in photo.

Center and sew Beak to center front of Bootie to rem lps of rnd 15.

DUCK BIB
Rnd 1: With size G hook and gold, ch 4, 13 dc in 4th ch from hook, **join** *(see Pattern Notes)* in 4th ch of beg ch-4. *(14 dc)*

Rnd 2: Ch 3 *(see Pattern Notes)*, dc in same st, 2 dc in each dc around, join in 3rd ch of beg ch-3. *(28 dc)*

Rnd 3: Ch 3, dc in same st, [dc in each of next 2 dc, 2 dc in next st] 9 times, join in 3rd ch of beg ch-3. *(38 dc)*

Rnd 4: Ch 3, dc in same st, [dc in each of next 3 dc, 2 dc in next dc] 9 times, dc in last dc, join in 3rd ch of beg ch-3. Fasten off. *(48 dc)*

Rnd 5: Join sunburst with sc in any dc of rnd 4, sc in each st around, join in beg sc. Fasten off. *(48 sc)*

EYE
MAKE 2.
With size G hook and chocolate, ch 2, 7 sc in 2nd ch from hook, join in beg sc. Leaving a long end, fasten off.

Sew Eyes between rnds 2 and 3 of Bib as shown in photo.

BEAK
Rnds 1 & 2: With dark yellow, rep rnds 1 and 2 of Bib. At the end of last rnd, sl st in next st. Leaving long end, fasten off.

With WS tog, fold Beak in half, sew across the fold, and then sew fold to center of Bib.

TIE
MAKE 2.
With size G hook, join sunburst with sl st in last rnd of Bib above Eye, ch 45, sl st in 2nd ch from hook, sl st in each ch across, sl st in same st on Bib as first sl st. Fasten off.

HAIR
Cut 2 lengths each of gold and sunburst 4 inches long. Holding 1 strand of each color tog, fold in half, working in 2 sts centered between Ties, insert hook in first st, pull strands through at fold to form lp on hook, pull ends through lp on hook. With rem 2 strands, attach in next st in same manner. ∎

Roomy Romper

DESIGN BY **DIANE SIMPSON**

SKILL LEVEL

■■■◻
INTERMEDIATE

FINISHED SIZES

Instructions given for size newborn–3 month, with changes for 6 months, 9 months and 12 months in [ ]

MATERIALS

- Bernat Baby Coordinates Sweet Stripes light (light worsted) weight yarn (5 oz/404 yds/150g per skein): 2 [2, 3, 3] skeins #09712 sprite stripes
- Sizes G/6/4mm and I/9/5.5mm crochet hooks or sizes needed to obtain gauge
- Tapestry needle
- Sewing needle
- Sewing thread
- White strip hook-and-loop fastener: 26 [28, 30, 32] inches
- ⅝-inch buttons: 2 [3, 3, 4]

GAUGE

Size G hook: 4 sc = 1 inch; 4 sc rows = 1 inch
Size I hook: 13 pattern sts = 4 inches; 12 pattern rows = 4 inches

INSTRUCTIONS
ROMPER
RIGHT FRONT YOKE

Row 1: Beg at armhole, with size I hook, ch 13 [15, 15, 17], sc in 2nd ch from hook, dc in next ch, [sc in next ch, dc in next ch] across, turn. *(12 [14, 14, 16] sts)*

Rows 2–4 [2–6, 2–6, 2–8]: Ch 1, sc in first st, dc in next st, [sc in next st, dc in next st] across, turn.

NECK SHAPING

Row 5 [7, 7, 9]: Ch 1, sc in first st, [dc in next st, sc in next st] 3 [4, 4, 5] times, **dc dec** (*see Stitch Guide*) in next 2 sts, leave rem sts unworked, turn. (*8 [10, 10, 12] sts*)

Row 6 [8, 8, 10]: Ch 1, **sc dec** (*see Stitch Guide*) in first 2 sts, [sc in next st, dc in next st] across, turn. (*7 [9, 9, 11] sts*)

Row 7 [9, 9, 11]: Ch 1, sc in first st, dc in next st, [sc in next st, dc in next st] across with dc in last st, turn.

Row 8 [10, 10, 12]: Ch 1, sc dec in first 2 sts, dc in next st, [sc in next st, dc in next st] across, turn. (*6 [8, 8, 10] sts*)

Row 9 [11, 11, 13]: Ch 1, sc in first st, dc in next st, [sc in next st, dc in next st] across. Fasten off.

RIGHT FRONT PLACKET

Row 10 [12, 12, 14] (RS): With size G hook, join sc in first st of last row, sc in same st, sc in each of next 2 sts, 2 sc in next st, sc in each st across, turn. (*8 [10, 10, 12] sc*)

Rows 11–13 [13–15, 13–17, 15–17]: Ch 1, sc in each st across, turn.

NEWBORN–3 MONTH SIZE ONLY

Row 14: Ch 1, sc in first st, [ch 1 (*buttonhole*), sk next st, sc in each of next 2 sts] twice, sc in last st, turn. (*2 buttonholes, 6 sc*)

6 MONTH & 9 MONTH SIZES ONLY

Row [16, 18]: Ch 1, sc in first st, [ch 1 (*buttonhole*), sk next st, sc in each of next 2 sts] across, turn. (*[3, 3] buttonholes, [7, 7] sc*)

12 MONTH SIZE ONLY

Row [18]: Ch 1, sc in first st, [ch 1 (*buttonhole*), sk next st, sc in each of next 2 sts] 3 times, ch 1, sk next st, sc in last st, turn. (*4 buttonholes, 8 sc*)

ALL SIZES

Row 15 [17, 19, 19]: Ch 1, sc in each st and in each ch across. Fasten off. (*8 [10, 10, 12] sc*)

LEFT FRONT YOKE

Rows 1–8 [1–10, 1–10, 1–12]: Rep rows 1–8 [1–10, 1–10, 1–12] of Right Front Yoke.

Row 9 [11, 11, 13]: Ch 1, sc in first st, dc in next st, [sc in next st, dc in next st] across, turn.

LEFT FRONT PLACKET

Row 10 [12, 12, 14] (RS): With size G hook, ch 1, sc in each st across to last 4 sts, 2 sc in next st, sc in each of next 2 sts, 2 sc in last st, turn. (*8 [10, 10, 12] sc*)

Rows 11–13 [13–15, 13–17, 15–17]: Ch 1, sc in each st across, turn. At end of last row, fasten off.

BACK YOKE
MAKE 2.

Row 1: Beg at armhole, with size I hook, ch 13 [15, 15, 17], sc in 2nd ch from hook, dc in next ch, [sc in next ch, dc in next ch] across, turn. (*12 [14, 14, 16] sts*)

Rows 2–4 [2–6, 2–6, 2–8]: Ch 1, sc in first st, dc in next st, [sc in next st, dc in next st] across, turn.

Row 5 [7, 7, 9]: Ch 1, sc in first st, [dc in next st, sc in next st] across to last 3 sts, dc dec in next 2 sts, leave last st unworked, turn. (*10 [12, 12, 15] sts*)

Row 6 [8, 8, 10]: Ch 1, sc in first st, dc in next st, [sc in next st, dc in next st] across, turn.

Row 7 [9, 9, 11]: Ch 1, sc in first st, [dc in next st, sc in next st] across to last 3 sts, dc dec in next 2 sts, leave last st unworked, turn. (*8 [10, 10, 12] sts*)

Rows 8–13 [10–15, 10–17, 12–17]: Ch 1, sc in first st, dc in next st, [sc in next st, dc in next st] across, turn. At end of last row, fasten off.

RIGHT FRONT BOTTOM

Row 1: With RS facing and size I hook, join with sc in first st at end of row 1 on Right Front Yoke at bottom, working in ends of rows, evenly sp 13 [16, 16, 20] sc across, leaving last 3 rows on placket unworked on all sizes, turn. (*14 [17, 17, 21] sc*)

NEWBORN–3 MONTH SIZE ONLY

Row 2: Ch 1, sc in first st, dc in next st, [(sc, dc) in each of next 2 sts, sc in next st, dc in next st] across, turn. (*20 sts*)

6 MONTH, 9 MONTH & 12 MONTH SIZES ONLY

Row [2]: Ch 1, sc in first st, dc in next st, sc in next st, dc in next st, [(sc, dc) in each of next 2 sts, sc in next st, dc in next st] [2, 2, 3] times, (sc, dc) in next st, [sc in next st, dc in next st] across, turn. ([22, 22, 28] sts)

FOR ALL SIZES

Rows 3–20 [3–22, 3–22, 3–24]: Ch 1, sc in first st, dc in next st, [sc in next st, dc in next st] across, turn.

Row 21 [23, 23, 25]: Ch 1, sc in first st, [dc in next st, sc in next st] across with 2 dc in last st, turn. (21 [23, 23, 29] sts)

Row 22 [24, 24, 26]: Ch 1, (sc, dc) in first st, [sc in next st, dc in next st] across, turn. (22 [24, 24, 30] sts)

Row 23 [25, 25, 27]: Ch 1, sc in first st, [dc in next st, sc in next st] across with 3 dc in last st, turn. (24 [26, 26, 32] sts)

Rows 24–26 [26–28, 26–30, 28–30]: Ch 1, sc in first st, dc in next st, [sc in next st, dc in next st] across, turn.

Row 27 [29, 31, 31]: Ch 1, sc dec in first 2 sts, [sc in next st, dc in next st] across, turn. (23 [25, 25, 31] sts)

Row 28 [30, 32, 32]: Ch 1, sc in first st, [dc in next st, sc in next st] across with sc dec in last 2 sts, turn. (22 [24, 24, 30] sts)

Rows 29 & 30 [31 & 32, 33 & 34, 33 & 34]: Ch 1, sc in first st, dc in next st, [sc in next st, dc in next st] across, turn.

Rows 31 & 32 [33 & 34, 35 & 36, 35 & 36]: Rep rows 27 and 28 [29 and 30, 31 and 32, 31 and 32]. (20 [22, 22, 28] sts at end of last row)

Rows 33 & 34 [35 & 36, 37 & 38, 37 & 38]: Ch 1, sc in first st, dc in next st, [sc in next st, dc in next st] across, turn.

Rows 35 & 36 [37 & 38, 39 & 40, 39 & 40]: Rep rows 27 and 28 [29 and 30, 31 and 32, 31 and 32]. (18 [20, 20, 26] sts at end of last row)

Rows 37–40 [39–42, 41 & 42, 41 & 42]: Ch 1, sc in first st, dc in next st, [sc in next st, dc in next st] across, turn.

Rows 41 & 42 [43 & 44, 43 & 44, 43 & 44]: Rep rows 27 and 28 [29 and 30, 31 and 32, 31 and 32]. (16 [18, 18, 24] sts at end of last row)

Rows 43–50 [45–51, 45 & 46, 45 & 46]: Ch 1, sc in first st, dc in next st, [sc in next st, dc in next st] across, turn.

NEWBORN–3 MONTH & 6 MONTH SIZES ONLY

At end of last row, fasten off.

9 MONTH & 12 MONTH SIZES ONLY

Rows [47 & 48, 47 & 48]: Rep rows [31 and 32, 31 and 32]. ([16, 22] sts at end of last row)

Rows [49–51, 49 & 50]: Ch 1, sc in first st, dc in next st, [sc in next st, dc in next st] across, turn.

9 MONTH SIZE ONLY

At end of last row, fasten off.

12 MONTH SIZE ONLY

Rows [51 & 52]: Rep rows [31] and [32]. ([20] sts at end of last row)

Row [53]: Ch 1, sc in first st, dc in next st, [sc in next st, dc in next st] across. Fasten off.

LEFT FRONT BOTTOM
FOR ALL SIZES

Row 1: With WS facing and size I hook, join with sc in first st at end of row 1 on Left Front Yoke at bottom, working in ends of rows, evenly sp 13 [16, 16, 20] sc across, leaving last 3 rows on placket unworked on all sizes, turn. (14 [17, 17, 21] sc)

Rows 2–50 [2–51, 2–51, 2–53]: Rep rows 2–50 [2–51, 2–51, 2–53] of Right Front Bottom.

FIRST BACK BOTTOM

Row 1: With size I hook, join sc in first st at end of row 1 on 1 Back Yoke at bottom and working in ends of rows, evenly sp 14 [16, 18, 18] sc across, turn. (15 [17, 19, 19] sts)

Row 2: Ch 1, sc in first st, dc in next st, *(sc, dc) in each of next 3 sts, sc in next st, dc in next st*, rep between * across to last 3 sts, (sc, dc) in next st, sc in next st, dc in last st for **Newborn–3 month size**, rep between * across for **6 month size**, rep between * across to last 2 sts, sc in next st, dc in next st for **9 month and 12 month sizes**, turn. *(22 [26, 28, 28] sts)*

Rows 3–21 [3–23, 3–23, 3–25]: Ch 1, sc in first st, dc in next st, [sc in next st, dc in next st] across, turn.

Row 22 [24, 24, 26]: Ch 3 *(counts as first dc)*, (2 dc, sc) in same st, dc in next st, [sc in next st, dc in next st] across, turn. *(25 [29, 31, 31] sts)*

Row 23 [25, 25, 27]: Ch 1, sc in first st, dc in next st, [sc in next st, dc in next st] across with 2 dc in last st, turn. *(26 [30, 32, 32] sts)*

Rows 24 & 25 [26 & 27, 26 & 27, 28 & 29]: Rep rows 22 and 23 [24 and 25, 24 and 25, 26 and 27] once. *(28 [34, 36, 36] sts at end of last row)*

Row 26 [28, 28, 30]: Ch 1, sc in first st, dc in next st, [sc in next st, dc in next st] across, turn.

Row 27 [29, 29, 31]: Ch 1, sc dec in first 2 sts, [sc in next st, dc in next st] across, turn. *(27 [33, 35, 35] sts)*

Row 28 [30, 30, 32]: Ch 1, sc in first st, [dc in next st, sc in next st] across with dc dec in last 2 sts, turn. *(26 [32, 34, 34] sts)*

Rows 29 & 30 [31 & 32, 31 & 34, 33 & 34]: Ch 1, sc in first st, dc in next st, [sc in next st, dc in next st] across, turn.

Rows 31 & 32 [33 & 34, 35 & 36, 35 & 36]: Rep rows 27 and 28 [29 and 30, 29 and 30, 31 and 32]. *(24 [30, 32, 32] sts at end of last row)*

Rows 33 & 34 [35 & 36, 37 & 38, 37 & 38]: Ch 1, sc in first st, dc in next st, [sc in next st, dc in next st] across, turn.

Rows 35 & 36 [37 & 38, 39 & 40, 39 & 40]: Rep rows 27 and 28 [29 and 30, 29 and 30, 31 and 32]. *(22 [28, 30, 30] sts at end of last row)*

Rows 37–40 [39–42, 41 & 42, 41 & 42]: Ch 1, sc in first st, dc in next st, [sc in next st, dc in next st] across, turn.

Rows 41 & 42 [43 & 44, 43 & 44, 43 & 44]: Rep rows 27 and 28 [29 and 30, 29 and 30, 31 and 32]. *(20 [26, 28, 28] sts at end of last row)*

Rows 43–50 [45–51, 45 & 46, 45 & 46]: Ch 1, sc in first st, dc in next st, [sc in next st, dc in next st] across, turn.

NEWBORN–3 MONTH & 6 MONTH SIZES ONLY
At end of last row, fasten off.

9 MONTH & 12 MONTH SIZES ONLY
Rows [47 & 48, 47 & 48]: Rep rows [29 and 30, 31 and 32]. *([26, 26] sts at end of last row)*

Rows [49–51, 49 & 50]: Ch 1, sc in first st, dc in next st, [sc in next st, dc in next st] across, turn.

9 MONTH SIZE ONLY
At end of last row, fasten off.

12 MONTH SIZE ONLY
Rows [51 & 52]: Rep rows [31] and [32]. *([24] sts at end of last row)*

Row [53]: Ch 1, sc in first st, dc in next st, [sc in next st, dc in next st] across. Fasten off.

2ND BACK BOTTOM
Rows 1–50 [1–51, 1–51, 1–53]: With size I hook and beg at bottom of 2nd Back Yoke, rep rows 1–50 [1–51, 1–51, 1–53] of Right Back Bottom.

FIRST SLEEVE
Sew Left Front Yoke and Left Back Yoke tog at shoulder seam.

Row 1: With size I hook, working in starting ch on opposite side of row 1 on Left Front Yoke, join with sc in first ch at end of row 1, sc in each st across, sk shoulder seam, sc in each ch across Left Back Yoke, turn. *(24 [28, 28, 32] sc)*

Row 2: Ch 1, sc dec in first 2 sts, [dc in next st, sc in next st] across with dc dec in last 2 sts, turn. *(22 [26, 26, 30] sts)*

Rows 3–5 [3–5, 3–7, 3–7]: Ch 1, sc in first st, dc in next st, [sc in next st, dc in next st] across, turn.

Row 6 [6, 8, 8]: Ch 1, sc dec in first 2 sts, [sc in next st, dc in next st] across with dc dec in last 2 sts, turn. *(20 [24, 24, 28] sts)*

Rows 7–9 [7–9, 9–11, 9–11]: Ch 1, sc in first st, [dc in next st, sc in next st] across with dc in each of last 2 sts, turn.

Row 10 [10, 12, 12]: Ch 1, sc dec in first 2 sts, [dc in next st, sc in next st] across with dc dec in last 2 sts, turn. *(18, [22, 22, 26] sts)*

Rows 11–13 [11–13, 13–15, 13–15]: Ch 1, sc in first st, dc in next st, [sc in next st, dc in next st] across, turn.

Row 14 [14, 16, 16]: Ch 1, sc dec in first 2 sts, [sc in next st, dc in next st] across with dc dec in last 2 sts, turn. *(16 [20, 20, 24] sts)*

Rows 15–17 [15–17, 17–19, 17–19]: Ch 1, sc in first st, [dc in next st, sc in next st] across with dc in each of last 2 sts, turn.

Row 18 [18, 20, 20]: Ch 1, sc dec in first 2 sts, [dc in next st, sc in next st] across with dc dec in last 2 sts, turn. *(14 [18, 18, 22] sts)*

Rows 19–21 [19–21, 21–23, 21–23]: Ch 1, sc in first st, dc in next st, [sc in next st, dc in next st] across, turn.

Row 22 [22, 24, 24]: Ch 1, sc dec in first 2 sts, [sc in next st, dc in next st] across with dc dec in last 2 sts, turn. *(12 [16, 16, 20] sts)*

Rows 23–25 [23–25, 25–27, 25–27]: Ch 1, sc in first st, [dc in next st, sc in next st] across with dc in each of last 2 sts, turn. At end of last row, fasten off.

2ND SLEEVE

Sew Right Front Yoke and Right Back Yoke tog at shoulder seam.

Row 1: With size I hook, working in starting ch on opposite side of row 1 on Right Back Yoke, join with sc in first ch at end of row 1, sc in each st across, sk shoulder seam, sc in each ch across Right Front Yoke, turn. *(24 [28, 28, 32] sc)*

Rows 2–25 [2–25, 2–27, 2–27]: Rep rows 2–25 [2–25, 2–27, 2–27] of First Sleeve.

ASSEMBLY

Sew underarm and side seams.

Matching ends of rows on Right and Left Fronts at center, overlapping plackets so Fronts will fit tog, sew center seam from row 1 at Bottoms through row 23 [25, 25, 27].

Matching ends of rows on Right and Left Back at center, sew center seam from top of Yoke down through row 23 [25, 25, 27] on Bottoms.

LEG FRONT CLOSURE PLACKET

Row 1: Working in ends of rows, with size G hook, join with sc in end of last row of Right Front Leg, evenly sp sc across to bottom of Left Front Leg, sc in each sc and 2 sc in each dc row across, turn.

Rows 2–4: Ch 1, sc in each st across, turn. At end of last row, fasten off.

FIRST CUFF

Row 1: With WS facing and working in sts of last row on 1 Leg, with size G hook, join in first st, ch 6, sc in 2nd ch from hook and in each ch across, sl st in each of next 2 sts on last row of Leg, turn. *(5 sc)*

Row 2: Working in **back lps** (see Stitch Guide), ch 1, sc in each sc across, turn.

Row 3: Working in back lps, ch 1, sc in each sc across, sl st in each of next 2 sts on last row of Leg, turn.

Row 4: Working in back lps, ch 1, sc in each st across, turn.

Next rows: Rep rows 3 and 4 alternately across Leg and Leg Front Closure Placket. At end of last row, fasten off.

2ND CUFF

Work in sts on last row of 2nd Leg, rep First Cuff.

Sew hook-and-loop fastener across center Leg
opening from 1 Cuff across to other Cuff.

NECK TRIM

Row 1: With RS facing and working in ends of
rows around neck opening, with size G hook,
join with sc in end of last row of Right Front
Placket, sc in end of each row and in each
st around to last row of Left Front Placket,
working [sc dec in next 2 sts] in sts on each side
of both shoulder seams, turn.

Rows 2 & 3: Ch 1, sc in each st across with [sc
dec in next 2 sts] in decreases on last row, turn.

Row 4: Working from left to right, ch 1, **reverse
sc** *(see Fig. 1)* in first st and in each st across.
Fasten off.

Sew buttons opposite buttonholes on Left Front
Placket. ∎

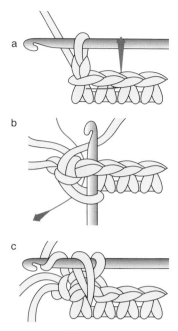

Fig. 1
Reverse Single Crochet

Primary Colors

CIRCUS STAR AFGHAN
DESIGN BY **JOHANNA DZIKOWSKI**

SKILL LEVEL
INTERMEDIATE

FINISHED SIZE
45 inches across

MATERIALS
- Red Heart Super Saver medium (worsted) weight yarn (7 oz/ 364 yds/198g per skein):
    1 skein each #324 bright yellow, #368 paddy green, #319 cherry red and #385 royal
- Size P/15/10mm crochet hook or size needed to obtain gauge

GAUGE
10 dc = 4 inches; 4 dc rows = 2½ inches

PATTERN NOTES
Chain-3 at beginning of row or round counts as first double crochet unless otherwise stated.

Join with slip stitch as indicated unless otherwise stated.

SPECIAL STITCHES
Shell: (2 dc, ch 2, 2 dc) in place indicated.
Picot: Ch 4, sl st in 4th ch from hook.

INSTRUCTIONS
AFGHAN
Rnd 1: With bright yellow, ch 5, sl st in first ch to form ring, **ch 3** (see Pattern Notes), 15 dc in ring, **join** (see Pattern Notes) in 3rd ch of beg ch-3. (16 dc)

Rnd 2: Ch 1, sc in first st, ch 4, sk next st, [sc in next st, ch 4, sk next st] around, join in beg sc. (8 sc, 8 ch-4 sps)

Rnd 3: Shell (see Special Stitches) in next ch sp, [sl st in next st, shell in next ch sp] around, join in joining sl st on last rnd. (8 sl sts, 8 shells)

Rnd 4: Sl st in each of next 2 sts, ch 3, *shell in next ch sp, dc in next st, sk next dc, next sl st and next dc**, dc in next st, rep from * around, ending last rep at **, join in 3rd ch of beg ch-3. (16 dc, 8 shells)

Rnd 5: Sl st in next st, ch 3, dc in next st, *shell in next ch sp, dc in each of next 2 sts, sk next 2 sts**, dc in each of next 2 sts, rep from * around, ending last rep at **, join in 3rd ch of beg ch-3. (32 dc, 8 shells)

Rnd 6: Sl st in next st, ch 3, dc in each of next 2 sts, *shell in next ch sp, dc in each of next 3 sts, sk next 2 sts**, dc in each of next 3 sts, rep from * around, ending last rep at **, join in 3rd ch of beg ch-3. Fasten off.

Rnd 7: Join paddy green in 2nd st, ch 3, dc in each st across to next ch sp, *shell in next ch sp, dc in each st across to 2 sts at next indentation, sk next 2 sts**, dc in each st across to next ch sp, rep from * around, ending last rep at **, join in 3rd ch of beg ch-3.

Rnd 8: Sl st in next st, ch 3, dc in each st across to next ch sp, *shell in next ch sp, dc in each st across to 2 sts at next indentation, sk next 2 sts**, dc in each st across to next ch sp, rep from * around, ending last rep at **, join in 3rd ch of beg ch-3.

Rnds 9–11: Sl st in next st, ch 3, dc in each st across to next ch sp, *shell in next ch sp, dc in each st across to 2 sts at next indentation, sk next 2 sts**, dc in each st across to next ch sp, rep from * around, ending last rep at **, join in 3rd ch of beg ch-3. At end of last rnd, fasten off.

Rnd 12: With cherry red, rep rnd 7.

Rnds 13–16: Rep rnd 8. At end of last rnd, fasten off.

Rnd 17: With royal, rep rnd 6.

Rnds 18–21: Rep rnd 8. At end of last rnd, fasten off.

Rnd 22: With bright yellow, rep rnd 7.

Rnds 23–25: Rep rnd 8. At end of last rnd, **turn**.

Rnd 26: Sl st in each of next 2 sts, ch 3, dc in each st across to next ch sp, *shell in next ch sp, dc in each st across to 2 sts at next indentation, sk next 2 sts**, dc in each st across to next ch sp, rep from * around, ending last rep at **, join in 3rd ch of beg ch-3. Fasten off.

ZAPPY ZIP-UPS
ORIGINAL BY **ANNIE**

SKILL LEVEL

INTERMEDIATE

FINISHED SIZES
Instructions given for size 6 months, with
changes for 12 months and 18 months in [ ].

MATERIALS
- Red Heart Sport light (light
  worsted) weight yarn (2½ oz/
  165 yds/70g per skein):
    2 skeins #846 skipper blue
    1 [1, 2] skeins each #687 paddy green
    and #912 cherry red
- Red Heart Designer Sport light (light worsted)
  weight yarn (3 oz/279 yds/85g per ball):
    1 ball #3215 lemon zest
- Size H/8/5mm crochet hook
  or size needed to obtain gauge
- Tapestry needle
- Sewing needle
- Sewing thread
- ¾-inch wide elastic: ½ yd
- ⅝-inch decorative buttons: 5
- Stitch markers

GAUGE
7 dc = 2 inches; 2 dc rows = 1 inch

PATTERN NOTES
Chain-3 at beginning of row or rounds counts as
first double crochet unless otherwise stated.

Join with slip stitch as indicated unless
otherwise stated.

INSTRUCTIONS
PANTS
LEG
MAKE 2.
Row 1: Beg at ankle, with skipper blue, ch 34
[36, 38], dc in 4th ch from hook (*first 3 chs
count as first dc*) and in each ch across, turn.
(*32 [34, 36] dc*)

Row 2: Ch 3 (*see Pattern Notes*), dc in each st
across, turn.

Row 3: Ch 3, dc in same st, dc in each st across
with 2 dc in last st, turn. (*34 [36, 38] dc*)

Next rows: [Rep rows 2 and 3 alternately]
5 [6, 7] times. (*44 [48, 52] dc at end of last row*)

Next row: Sl st in each of first 3 sts (*crotch
shaping*), ch 3, dc in each st across, leaving last
2 sts unworked, turn. (*40 [44, 48] dc*)

Next row: Ch 3, **dc dec** (*see Stitch Guide*) in next
2 sts, dc in each st across to last 3 sts, dc dec in
next 2 sts, dc in last st, turn. (*38 [42, 46] dc*)

Next row: Ch 3, dc in each st across, turn.

Next rows: Rep last 2 rows 5 [6, 6] times.
(*28 [30, 34] dc at end of last rnd*)

Next rows: Rep row 2 until Leg measures 8
[8½, 9] inches from crotch. At end of last rnd,
fasten off.

WAISTBAND
Next row: Join paddy green with sc at right-
hand side of top with RS facing, sc in each
st across, turn.

Next row: Ch 1, sc in each st across, turn.

Next row: Rep last row until Waistband measures 1½ inches. At end of last row, fasten off.

LEG RIBBING
Row 1: Working in starting ch on opposite side of row 1, **join** (*see Pattern Notes*) paddy green in first ch, ch 3, dc in each ch across, turn.

Rows 2–4: Ch 3, **bpdc** (*see Stitch Guide*) around next st, [**fpdc** (*see Stitch Guide*) around next st, bpdc around next st] across, turn. At end of last row, fasten off.

FINISHING
Sew Leg and Ribbing seams. Sew crotch seam.

Turn Waistband down at front over 1½ inches toward Leg, sew in place, leaving small opening in back for elastic.

Weave elastic through Waistband, overlap ends and sew tog.

Sew opening closed.

CARDIGAN
BACK
Row 1: With cherry red, ch 40 [42, 46], dc in 4th ch from hook (*first 3 chs count as first dc*) and in each ch across, turn. (*38 [40, 44] dc*)

Row 2: Ch 3, dc in each st across, turn.

Next rows: Rep row 2 until piece measures 4½ [5½, 6½] inches from beg.

ARMHOLE SHAPING
Next row: Sl st in each of first 3 [3, 4] sts, ch 3, dc in each st across, leaving last 2 [2, 3] sts unworked, turn. (*34 [36, 38] dc*)

Next row: Ch 3, dc dec in next 2 sts, dc in each st across to last 3 sts, dc dec in next 2 sts, dc in last st, turn. (*32 [34, 36] dc*)

Next rows: Rep last row 8 [9, 10] times. At end of last row, fasten off. (*16 [16, 16] dc at end of last row*)

BOTTOM RIBBING
Row 1: Working in starting ch on opposite side of row 1, join paddy green in first ch, ch 3, dc in each ch across, turn. (*34 [36, 38] dc*)

Rows 2 & 3: Ch 3, bpdc around next st, [fpdc around next st, bpdc around next st] across. At end of last row, fasten off.

FIRST FRONT
Row 1: With cherry red, ch 20 [21, 23], dc in 4th ch from hook (*first 3 chs count as first dc*) and in each ch across, turn. (*18 [19, 21] dc*)

Next rows: Work same as Back up to Armhole Shaping.

ARMHOLE SHAPING
Next row: Sl st in each of first 3 [3, 4] sts, ch 3, dc in each st across turn. (*16 [17, 18] dc*)

Next row: Ch 3, dc in each st across to last 3 sts, dc dec in next st, dc in last st, turn. (*15 [16, 17] dc*)

Next row: Ch 3, dc dec in next 2 sts, dc in each st across, turn. (*14 [15, 16] dc*)

Next rows: Rep last 2 rows 3 [3, 4] times. At end of last row, fasten off. (*8 [9, 8] dc at end of last row*)

NECK SHAPING
Next row: Sl st in each of first 7 [8, 7] sts, ch 3, dc in last st, turn. (*2 dc*)

Last row: Ch 3, dc in last st. Fasten off.

BOTTOM RIBBING
Row 1: Working in starting ch on opposite side of row 1, join paddy green in first ch, ch 3, dc in each ch across, turn.

Rows 2 & 3: Ch 3, bpdc around next 1 [0, 0] st, [fpdc around next st, bpdc around next st] across. At end of last row, fasten off.

2ND FRONT
Work same as First Front, reversing all shaping.

RAGLAN SLEEVE
MAKE 2.

Row 1: With lemon zest, ch 25 [27, 29], dc in 4th ch from hook *(first 3 chs count as first dc)* and in each ch across, turn. *(23 [25, 27] dc)*

Row 2: Ch 3, dc in each st across, turn.

Row 3: Ch 3, 2 dc in next st, dc in each st across with 2 dc in last st, turn. *(25 [27, 29] dc)*

Rows 4 & 5: Rep row 3 twice. *(29 [31, 33] dc at end of last row)*

Next rows: Rep row 2 until Sleeve measures 6 [6½, 7] inches from beg.

SLEEVE SHAPING

Next row: Sl st in each of first 3 sts, ch 3, dc in each st across, leaving last 2 sts unworked, turn. *(27 [29, 31] dc)*

Next row: Ch 3, dc dec in next 2 sts, dc in each st across to last 3 sts, dc dec in next 2 sts, dc in last st, turn. *(25 [27, 29] sts)*

Next rows: Rep last row 10 [10, 10] times. At end of last row, fasten off. *(5 [7, 9] dc at end of last row)*

Last row, when sewn to Fronts and Back, will be part of neck edge.

SLEEVE RIBBING

Row 1: Working in starting ch on opposite side of row 1, join paddy green in first ch, ch 3, dc in each ch across, turn.

Rows 2 & 3: Ch 3, [fpdc around next st, bpdc around next st] across. At end of last row, fasten off.

FINISHING

Sew Sleeves to Armholes on Fronts and Back.

Sew side and Sleeve seams.

NECK EDGING

Row 1: With RS facing, working in sts across Fronts, Back and Sleeves, join paddy green in first st on Front, ch 3, dc in each st across, turn.

Rows 2 & 3: Ch 3, bpdc around next st, [fpdc around next st, bpdc around next st] across. At end of last row, fasten off.

BUTTON BAND

Row 1: On left side for girls and right side for boys, working in ends of rows across Bottom Ribbing, Front edge and Neck Ribbing, join paddy green with sc in end of first row, evenly sp sc across so piece lies flat, turn.

Rows 2 & 3: Ch 1, sc in each st across, turn. At end of last row, fasten off.

BUTTONHOLE BAND

Row 1: Working on rem Front in ends of rows, join paddy green with sc in first row, evenly sp sc across so piece lies flat, turn. Mark 5 places evenly spaced across for buttonholes.

Row 2: Ch 1, sc in each st across to marker, [ch 2, sk next 2 sts, sc in each st across to next marker] across, sc in each st across, turn.

Row 3: Ch 1, sc in each st and in each ch across. Fasten off.

Sew buttons to Button Band opposite buttonholes.

RUNNING SHOES
ORIGINAL BY **ANNIE**

SKILL LEVEL
INTERMEDIATE

FINISHED SIZE
Instructions given for 6 months (4-inch sole), with changes for 12 months (5-inch sole) in [ ].

MATERIALS
- Red Heart Sport light (light worsted) weight yarn (2½ oz/ 165 yds/70g per skein):
    1 skein each #687 paddy green, #912 cherry red and #846 skipper blue
- Red Heart Designer Sport light (light worsted) weight yarn (3 oz/279 yds/ 85g per ball):
    1 ball #3215 lemon zest
- Size hook listed with gauge for size or size needed to obtain gauge
- Tapestry needle

GAUGE
Size F/5/3.75mm hook (6 months): 18 sts = 4 inches; 5 rows = 1 inch
Size G/6/4mm hook (12 months): 16 sts = 4 inches; 4 rows = 1 inch

PATTERN NOTES
Join with slip stitch as indicated unless otherwise stated.

Chain-3 at beginning of row or round counts as first double crochet unless otherwise stated.

INSTRUCTIONS
SHOE
MAKE 2.
SOLE
Rnd 1: With paddy green, ch 15, 2 sc in 2nd ch from hook and in each of next 9 chs, hdc in each of next 3 chs, 6 hdc in last ch, working on

opposite side of ch, hdc in each of next 3 chs, sc in each of next 9 chs, 2 sc in last ch, **join** (see Pattern Notes) in beg sc. (32 sts)

Rnd 2: Ch 1, 2 sc in first st, sc in each st around with 2 sc in last st, join in beg sc. (36 sc)

Rnd 3: Ch 1, 2 sc in first st, sc in each of next 15 sts, 2 sc in each of next 4 sts, sc in each of next 15 sts, 2 sc in last st, join in beg sc. Fasten off. (42 sts)

Rnd 4: Working in **back lps** (see Stitch Guide), join skipper blue in first st, ch 3, dc in each st around, join in 3rd ch of beg ch-3. Fasten off.

TOE
Working in back lps, sk first 15 sts, join in next st, sc in next st, sk next st, dc in each of next 2 sts, **dc dec** (see Stitch Guide) in next 2 sts, dc in each of next 2 sts, sk next st, sc in next st, sl st in next st, leaving rem sts unworked. Fasten off.

TONGUE
Row 1: Working in back lps, join lemon zest in first sc on right hand side of Toe, sc in each st across Toe, turn. (7 sc)

Row 2: Working in both lps, ch 1, **sc dec** (see Stitch Guide) in first 2 sts, [sc dec in next 2 sts] twice, sc in last st, turn. (4 sc)

Rows 3–7: Ch 1, sc in each st across, turn. At end of last row, fasten off.

SIDES
Row 1: Working in back lps, join cherry red in same st on Toe as last st of row 1 on Tongue, sk next st on Sole, sc in each of next 30 sts around Sole, sk last st on Sole, sc in same st on Toe as the first st of Tongue, turn. (32 sc)

Row 2: Ch 1, sc in each st across, turn.

Row 3: Ch 1, sc in each of first 5 sts, leaving rem sts unworked, turn.

Row 4: Ch 1, sc in each st across, turn.

Row 5: Ch 1, sc in each of first 5 sts, sc in each st across row 2, leaving last 5 sts unworked, **do not fasten off**. Drop lp from hook.

Row 6: With separate ball of cherry red, join with sc in next unworked st on row 4, sc in each of last 4 sts, turn.

Row 7: Ch 1, sc in each of 5 sts. Fasten off.

Row 8: Pick up dropped lp, sc in each of next 5 sts on row 7. Fasten off.

CUFF
Rnd 1: Working in back lps, join paddy green with sc in first st at left of center back, sc in each st across, working in both lps, sc in each st across Tongue, working in back lps, sc in each rem st on Sides, join in beg sc.

Rnd 2: Ch 3 *(see Pattern Notes)* **fpdc** *(see Stitch Guide)* around each st around, join in 3rd ch of beg ch-3.

Rnds 3–5: Ch 3, **bpdc** *(see Stitch Guide)* around next st, [fpdc around next st, bpdc around next st] around, join in 3rd ch of beg ch-3. At end of last rnd, fasten off.

TIE
With paddy green, ch 70. Fasten off.

Lace Tie though sts at both ends of last row on Side. Tie in bow. ▪

BUNNY BUDDIES

POCKET PAL BLANKET
DESIGN BY **MICHELE MAKS**

SKILL LEVEL

INTERMEDIATE

FINISHED SIZE
39 inches square

MATERIALS
- Caron Simply Soft medium (worsted) weight yarn (3 oz/ 157 yds/85g per skein):
  3 skeins #2705 soft green
  2 skeins #2613 soft yellow
- Caron Simply Soft Brites medium (worsted) weight yarn (6 oz/315 yds/170g per skein):
  3 skeins #9606 lemonade
  2 skeins each #9605 mango and #9607 limelight
- Size H/8/5mm crochet hook or size needed to obtain gauge
- Tapestry needle

GAUGE
14 sc = 4 inches; 20 sc rows = 4 inches

PATTERN NOTE
Join with slip stitch as indicated unless otherwise stated.

INSTRUCTIONS
BLANKET
Row 1: With soft green, ch 131, sc in 2nd ch from hook and in each ch across, turn. (*130 sc*)

Row 2: Ch 1, sc in each st across. Fasten off.

Row 3: Join lemonade with sc in first st, sc in each st across, turn.

Row 4: Ch 1, sc in each st across, turn. Fasten off.

Row 5: Join soft green with sc in first st, sc in each st across, turn.

Row 6: Ch 1, sc in each st across, turn. Fasten off.

Rows 7–34: [Rep rows 3–6 consecutively] 7 times.

Row 35: Join mango with sc in first st, sc in each st across, turn.

Rows 36–38: Ch 1, sc in each st across, turn. At end of last row, fasten off.

Rows 39–70: With limelight and soft yellow, [rep rows 3 and 4 consecutively] 8 times.

Rows 71 & 72: With limelight, rep rows 3 and 4.

Rows 73–76: Rep rows 35–38.

Rows 77 & 78: Rep rows 5 and 6.

Rows 79–110: [Rep rows 3–6 consecutively] 8 times.

Rows 111–114: Rep rows 35–38.

Rows 115–146: With limelight and soft yellow, [rep rows 3 and 4 consecutively] 8 times.

Rows 147 & 148: With limelight, rep rows 3 and 4.

Rows 149–152: Rep rows 35–38.

Next rows: With soft green and lemonade, [rep rows 3 and 4 consecutively] 8 times.

Next rows: With soft green, rep rows 3 and 4.

EDGING
Rnd 1: Now working in rnds, join mango with sc in first st, 2 sc in same st *(corner)*, sc in each st across with 3 sc in last st *(corner)*, working in ends of rows, evenly sp sc across, working in starting ch on opposite side of row 1, 3 sc in first ch *(corner)*, sc in each ch across with 3 sc in last ch *(corner)*, working in ends of rows, evenly sp sc across, **join** *(see Pattern Note)*, in beg sc, **turn.**

Rnds 2–4: Ch 1, sc in each st around with 3 sc in each center corner st, join in beg sc. Fasten off.

POCKET
Rnd 1: With mango, ch 33, sc in 2nd ch from hook and in each ch across, turn. (32 sc)

Rows 2–110: Ch 1, sc in each st across, turn. At end of last row, fasten off.

EDGING
Rnd 1: Now working in rnds, join mango with sc in first st, 2 sc in same st *(corner)*, sc in each st across with 3 sc in last st *(corner)*, working in ends of rows, evenly sp sc across, working in starting ch on opposite side of row 1, 3 sc in first ch *(corner)*, sc in each ch across with 3 sc in last ch *(corner)*, working in ends of rows, evenly sp sc across, **join** *(see Pattern Note)*, in beg sc, **turn.**

Rnds 2–4: Ch 1, sc in each st around with 3 sc in each center corner st, join in beg sc. Fasten off.

FINISHING

Sew Pocket between 3 center stripe sections along side and about 7 inches from edge around 3 sides, leaving 1 long edge open for top.

To make pockets, sew down through pocket 8 inches from each side edge. This will form 3 pockets.

BUNNY POCKET PAL
DESIGN BY SHEILA LESLIE

SKILL LEVEL

INTERMEDIATE

FINISHED SIZE

6 inches high sitting, excluding Ears

MATERIALS

- Caron Simply Soft medium (worsted) weight yarn (3 oz/ 157 yds/198g per skein):
    1 skein #2613 soft yellow
    ½ oz/25 yds/14g each #2601 white and #2680 black
- Caron Simply Soft Brites medium (worsted) weight yarn (6 oz/315 yds/170g per skein):
    1 oz/50 yds/28g #9606 lemonade
- Size G/6/4mm crochet hook or size needed to obtain gauge
- Tapestry needle
- Fiberfill
- Stitch marker

4 MEDIUM

GAUGE

9 sc = 2 inches

PATTERN NOTE

Do not join or turn rounds unless otherwise stated.

Mark first stitch of each round.

Join with slip stitch as indicated unless otherwise stated.

SPECIAL STITCH

Cluster (cl): Holding back last lp of each st on hook, 3 dc in place indicated, yo, pull through all lps on hook.

INSTRUCTIONS
BUNNY
HEAD

Rnd 1: Beg at top of head with soft yellow, ch 2, 6 sc in 2nd ch from hook, **do not join** (*see Pattern Notes*). (*6 sc*)

Rnd 2: 2 sc in each st around. (*12 sc*)

Rnd 3: [Sc in next st, 2 sc in next st] around. (*18 sc*)

Rnd 4: [Sc in each of next 2 sts, 2 sc in next st] around. (*24 sc*)

Rnd 5: [Sc in each of next 5 sts, 2 sc in next st] around. (*28 sc*)

Rnd 6: Sc in each st around.

Rnd 7: [Sc in each of next 13 sts, 2 sc in next st] around. *(30 sc)*

Rnds 8–13: Sc in each st around. Stuff Head.

Rnd 14: [Sc in each of next 3 sts, **sc dec** *(see Stitch Guide)* in next 2 sts] around. *(24 sc)*

Rnd 15: [Sc in each of next 2 sts, sc dec in next 2 sts] around, **join** *(see Pattern Notes)* in beg sc. Fasten off.

BODY

Rnd 1: Leaving long end, with soft yellow, ch 18, sl st in first ch to form ring, sc in each ch around, **do not join**. *(18 sc)*

Rnd 2: [Sc in each of next 5 sts, 2 sc in next st] around. *(21 sc)*

Rnd 3: Sc in each st around.

Rnd 4: [Sc in each of next 6 sts, 2 sc in next st] around. *(24 sc)*

Rnd 5: [Sc in each of next 3 sts, 2 sc in next st] around. *(30 sc)*

Rnds 6–12: Sc in each st around.

Rnd 13: [Sc in each of next 3 sts, sc dec in next 2 sts] around. *(24 sc)*

Rnd 14: [Sc in each of next 2 sts, sc dec in next 2 sts] around. *(18 sc)*

Rnd 15: [Sc dec in next 2 sts] around. *(9 sc)*

Rnd 16: [Sc dec in next 2 sts] 4 times, sc in last st, join in beg sc. Leaving long end, fasten off.

Stuff Body.

Weave long end through top of sts on last rnd, pull to close. Secure end.

With long end at beg of Body, sew Head to Body.

CHEEK
MAKE 2.

Rnd 1: With soft yellow, ch 2, 6 sc in 2nd ch from hook, **do not join**. *(6 sc)*

Rnd 2: 2 sc in each st around. *(12 sc)*

Rnds 3 & 4: Sc in each st around. At end of last rnd, join in beg sc. Leaving long end, fasten off.

Stuff Cheeks and using long end, sew to lower part of Head as shown in photo.

NOSE

With lemonade, ch 3, **cl** *(see Special Stitch)* in 3rd ch from hook, ch 1, sl st in same ch. Fasten off.

Sew to Head between Cheeks as shown in photo.

EYES

Using **satin stitch** *(see Fig. 1)*, with black, embroider Eyes on Head above Cheeks as shown in photo.

Fig. 1
Satin Stitch

INNER EAR
MAKE 2.

With white, ch 10, sc in 2nd ch from hook and in each of next 3 chs, hdc in each of next 3 chs, dc in next ch, 3 dc in last ch, working on opposite side of ch, 3 dc in next ch, dc in next ch, hdc in each of next 3 chs, sc in each of last 4 chs. Fasten off.

OUTER EAR
MAKE 2.

Row 1: With soft yellow, ch 10, sc in 2nd ch from hook and in each of next 3 chs, hdc in each of next 3 chs, dc in next ch, 3 dc in last ch, working on opposite side of ch, 3 dc in next ch, dc in next ch, hdc in each of next 3 chs, sc in each of last 4 chs, turn.

Row 2: Holding 1 Inner Ear with RS facing on top of Outer Ear, working through both thicknesses, ch 1, sc in each of next 10 sts, 2 sc in next st, ch 1, 2 sc in next st, sc in each of last 10 sts. Fasten off.

Sew Ears to top of Head as shown in photo.

LEG
MAKE 2.

Rnd 1: Beg at foot, with lemonade, ch 2, 6 sc in 2nd ch from hook, **do not join**. *(6 sc)*

Rnd 2: 2 sc in first st, sc in next st, 2 hdc in each of next 2 sts, sc in next st, 2 sc in last st, turn. *(10 sts)*

Rnd 3: 2 sc in next st, sc in each of next 2 sts, 2 hdc in each of next 4 sts, sc in next st, 2 sc in next st, sc in last st, join in beg sc. Fasten off. *(16 sts)*

Rnd 4: Working in **back lps** *(see Stitch Guide)*, join soft yellow with sc in first st, sc in each st around.

Rnd 5: Sc in each of first 5 sts, [sc dec in next 2 sts] 3 times, sc in each of last 5 sts. *(13 sc)*

Rnd 6: Sc in each of first 5 sts, sc dec in next 2 sts, sc in each of last 6 sts. *(12 sc)*

Rnds 7 & 8: Sc in each st around.

Rnd 9: [Sc in each of next 2 sts, 2 sc in next st] around. *(16 sc)*

Rnd 10: [Sc in each of next 7 sts, 2 sc in next st] around, join in beg sc. Leaving long end, fasten off.

Stuff Legs.

Sew Legs to front of Body in sitting position as shown in photo.

ARM
MAKE 2.

Rnd 1: Beg at top with soft yellow, leaving long end, ch 11, sl st in first ch to form ring, sc in each ch around, **do not join**. *(11 sc)*

Rnds 2–6: Sc in each st around.

Rnd 7: Sc in each of first 4 sts, 2 sc in each of next 3 sts, sc in each of last 4 sts. *(14 sc)*

Rnds 8 & 9: Sc in each st around.

Rnd 10: [Sc in next st, sc dec in next 2 sts, sc in each of next 2 sts, sc dec in next 2 sts] around. *(10 sc)*

Rnd 11: [Sc dec in next 2 sts] around, join in beg sc. Leaving long end, fasten off.

Weave long end through top of sts on last rnd, pull to close. Secure end.

Stuff Arm, leaving first 3 rnds unstuffed.

Flatten rnd 1 and sew closed.

Sew Arms to Body as shown in photo.

TAIL
With soft yellow, work same as Cheek.

Stuff and sew to bottom on back of Body.

TUMMY PANEL
Row 1: Beg at bottom with lemonade, ch 3, sc in 2nd ch from hook, sc in next ch, turn. *(2 sc)*

Row 2: Ch 1, 2 sc in first st, sc in next st, turn. *(3 sc)*

Row 3: 2 sc in first st, sc in each of last 2 sts, turn. *(4 sc)*

Row 4: 2 sc in first st, sc in each of next 2 sts, 2 sc in last st, turn. *(6 sc)*

Rows 5–9: Sc in each st across, turn.

Row 10: Sc dec in first 2 sts, sc in each of next 2 sts, sc dec in next 2 sts. *(4 sc)*

Row 11: [Dc dec in next 2 sts] across, **do not turn**. *(2 sc)*

Row 12: Working in ends of rows, evenly sp 11 sc in ends of rows across side, work in starting ch on opposite side of row 1, 2 sc in first ch, sc in each ch across with 2 sc in last ch, evenly sp 11 sc in ends of rows across side, sl st in first st on row 10. Leaving long end, fasten off.

Sew Tummy Panel to front of Body with row 11 at neck.

FLOWER
DESIGN BY **DOROTHY BUICK**

SKILL LEVEL

INTERMEDIATE

FINISHED SIZE
2¼ inches across

MATERIALS
- Caron Simply Soft medium (worsted) weight yarn (3 oz/ 157 yds/198g per skein):
  ½ oz/25 yds/14g #2601 white
- Caron Simply Soft Brites medium (worsted) weight yarn (6 oz/315 yds/170g per skein):
  ½ oz/25 yds/14g #9605 mango
- Size G/6/4mm crochet hook
- Tapestry needle

GAUGE
Gauge is not important on this item.

PATTERN NOTE
Join with slip stitch as indicated unless otherwise stated.

INSTRUCTIONS
FLOWER
Rnd 1: With mango, ch 4, sl st in first ch to form ring, ch 1, 12 sc in ring, **join** (see Pattern Note) in beg sc. Fasten off. (12 sc)

Rnd 2: Join white in any sc, ch 6, [sl st in next st, ch 6] around, join in joining sl st of last rnd. Leaving long end, fasten off.

Using long end, sew Flower to front of Bunny as shown in photo.

BUNNY HAT
DESIGN BY **DOROTHY BUICK**

SKILL LEVEL
INTERMEDIATE

FINISHED SIZES
Instructions given for size newborn, with changes for 6 months and 12 months in [ ]

MATERIALS
- Caron Simply Soft medium (worsted) weight yarn (3 oz/ 157 yds/85g per skein):
  1 skein #2613 soft yellow
  ½ oz/25 yds/14g #2601 white
- Caron Simply Soft Brites medium (worsted) weight yarn (6 oz/315 yds/170g per skein):
  ½ oz/25 yds/14g #9605 mango
- Size G/6/4mm crochet hook or size needed to obtain gauge
- Tapestry needle

GAUGE
4 dc = 1 inch; 2 dc rnds = 1 inch

PATTERN NOTES

Join with slip stitch as indicated unless otherwise stated.

Chain-3 at beginning of row or round counts as first double crochet unless otherwise stated.

INSTRUCTIONS

HAT

Rnd 1: With soft yellow, ch 4, sl st in first ch to form ring, ch 4 *(counts as first tr)*, 15 tr in ring, **join** *(see Pattern Notes)* in 4th of beg ch-4. *(16 tr)*

Rnd 2: **Ch 3** *(see Pattern Notes)*, dc in same st, 2 dc in each st around, join in 3rd ch of beg ch-3. *(32 dc)*

Rnd 3: Ch 3, 2 dc in next st, [dc in next st, 2 dc in next st] around, join in 3rd ch of beg ch-3. *(48 dc)*

6 MONTH & 12 MONTH SIZES ONLY

Rnd [4]: Ch 3, dc in each of next [4, 1] sts, 2 dc in next st, *dc in each of next [5, 2] sts, 2 dc in next st, rep from * around, join in 3rd ch of beg ch-3. *([56, 64] dc)*

ALL SIZES

Rnds 4–10 [5–11, 5–13]: Ch 3, dc in each st around, join in 3rd ch of beg ch-3.

BRIM

Rnds 11–16 [12–17, 14–19]: Ch 1, sc in each st around, join in beg sc. At end of last rnd, fasten off.

EARS

Rnd 1: With soft yellow, ch 33, 6 sc in 2nd ch from hook, sc in each of next 13 chs, sl st in each of next 4 chs, sc in each of next 13 chs, 6 sc in last ch, working on opposite side of ch, sc in each of next 13 chs, sl st in each of next 4 sts, sc in each of last 13 sts, join in beg sc. *(72 sts)*

Rnd 2: Ch 2 *(counts as first hdc)*, hdc in same st, 2 hdc in each of next 5 sts, hdc in each of next 13 sts, sl st in each of next 4 sts, hdc in each of next 13 sts, 2 hdc in each of next 6 sts, hdc in each of next 13 sts, sl st in each of next 4 sts, hdc in each of next 13 sts, join in 2nd ch of beg ch-2. Fasten off. *(84 sts)*

Lace Ears through sts of rnd 1 on Hat, insert 1 end of Ears from outside to inside between 6th and 7th sts and then to outside between 9th and 10th sts, placing sl st section of Ears on inside of Hat and with RS of Ears facing.

FLOWER

Rnd 1: With mango, ch 4, sl st in first ch to form ring, ch 1, 12 sc in ring, **join** *(see Pattern Note)* in beg sc. Fasten off. *(12 sc)*

Rnd 2: Join white in any sc, ch 6, [sl st in next st, ch 6] around, join in joining sl st of last rnd. Leaving long end, fasten off.

Using long end, sew Flower to top of Hat over Ears as shown in photo. ■

Stitch Guide

For more complete information, visit **FreePatterns.com**

ABBREVIATIONS

beg	begin/begins/beginning
bpdc	back post double crochet
bpsc	back post single crochet
bptr	back post treble crochet
CC	contrasting color
ch(s)	chain(s)
ch-	refers to chain or space previously made (e.g., ch-1 space)
ch sp(s)	chain space(s)
cl(s)	cluster(s)
cm	centimeter(s)
dc	double crochet (singular/plural)
dc dec	double crochet 2 or more stitches together, as indicated
dec	decrease/decreases/decreasing
dtr	double treble crochet
ext	extended
fpdc	front post double crochet
fpsc	front post single crochet
fptr	front post treble crochet
g	gram(s)
hdc	half double crochet
hdc dec	half double crochet 2 or more stitches together, as indicated
inc	increase/increases/increasing
lp(s)	loop(s)
MC	main color
mm	millimeter(s)
oz	ounce(s)
pc	popcorn(s)
rem	remain/remains/remaining
rep(s)	repeat(s)
rnd(s)	round(s)
RS	right side
sc	single crochet (singular/plural)
sc dec	single crochet 2 or more stitches together, as indicated
sk	skip/skipped/skipping
sl st(s)	slip stitch(es)
sp(s)	space/spaces/spaced
st(s)	stitch(es)
tog	together
tr	treble crochet
trtr	triple treble
WS	wrong side
yd(s)	yard(s)
yo	yarn over

Chain—ch: Yo, pull through lp on hook.

Slip stitch—sl st: Insert hook in st, pull through both lps on hook.

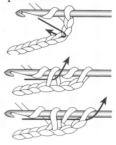

Single crochet—sc: Insert hook in st, yo, pull through st, yo, pull through both lps on hook.

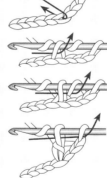

Front post stitch—fp: Back post stitch—bp: When working post st, insert hook from right to left around post st on previous row.

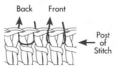

Front loop—front lp Back loop—back lp

Half double crochet— hdc: Yo, insert hook in st, yo, pull through st, yo, pull through all 3 lps on hook.

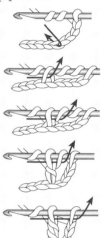

Double crochet—dc: Yo, insert hook in st, yo, pull through st, [yo, pull through 2 lps] twice.

Double treble crochet—dtr: Yo 3 times, insert hook in st, yo, pull through st, [yo, pull through 2 lps] 4 times.

Change colors: Drop first color; with 2nd color, pull through last 2 lps of st.

Treble crochet—tr: Yo twice, insert hook in st, yo, pull through st, [yo, pull through 2 lps] 3 times.

Single crochet decrease (sc dec): (Insert hook, yo, draw lp through) in each of the sts indicated, yo, draw through all lps on hook.

Example of 2-sc dec

Half double crochet decrease (hdc dec): (Yo, insert hook, yo, draw lp through) in each of the sts indicated, yo, draw through all lps on hook.

Example of 2-hdc dec

Double crochet decrease (dc dec): (Yo, insert hook, yo, draw loop through, draw through 2 lps on hook) in each of the sts indicated, yo, draw through all lps on hook.

Example of 2-dc dec

Treble crochet decrease (tr dec): Holding back last lp of each st, tr in each of the sts indicated, yo, pull through all lps on hook.

Example of 2-tr dec

US		UK
sl st (slip stitch)	=	sc (single crochet)
sc (single crochet)	=	dc (double crochet)
hdc (half double crochet)	=	htr (half treble crochet)
dc (double crochet)	=	tr (treble crochet)
tr (treble crochet)	=	dtr (double treble crochet)
dtr (double treble crochet)	=	ttr (triple treble crochet)
skip	=	miss

Metric
Conversion
Charts

METRIC CONVERSIONS

yards	x	.9144	=	metres (m)
yards	x	91.44	=	centimetres (cm)
inches	x	2.54	=	centimetres (cm)
inches	x	25.40	=	millimetres (mm)
inches	x	.0254	=	metres (m)

centimetres	x	.3937	=	inches
metres	x	1.0936	=	yards

INCHES INTO MILLIMETRES & CENTIMETRES (Rounded off slightly)

inches	mm	cm	inches	cm	inches	cm	inches	cm
1/8	3	0.3	5	12.5	21	53.5	38	96.5
1/4	6	0.6	5 1/2	14	22	56	39	99
3/8	10	1	6	15	23	58.5	40	101.5
1/2	13	1.3	7	18	24	61	41	104
5/8	15	1.5	8	20.5	25	63.5	42	106.5
3/4	20	2	9	23	26	66	43	109
7/8	22	2.2	10	25.5	27	68.5	44	112
1	25	2.5	11	28	28	71	45	114.5
1 1/4	32	3.2	12	30.5	29	73.5	46	117
1 1/2	38	3.8	13	33	30	76	47	119.5
1 3/4	45	4.5	14	35.5	31	79	48	122
2	50	5	15	38	32	81.5	49	124.5
2 1/2	65	6.5	16	40.5	33	84	50	127
3	75	7.5	17	43	34	86.5		
3 1/2	90	9	18	46	35	89		
4	100	10	19	48.5	36	91.5		
4 1/2	115	11.5	20	51	37	94		

KNITTING NEEDLES CONVERSION CHART

Canada/U.S.	0	1	2	3	4	5	6	7	8	9	10	10½	11	13	15
Metric (mm)	2	2¼	2¾	3¼	3½	3¾	4	4½	5	5½	6	6½	8	9	10

CROCHET HOOKS CONVERSION CHART

Canada/U.S.	1/B	2/C	3/D	4/E	5/F	6/G	8/H	9/I	10/J	10½/K	N
Metric (mm)	2.25	2.75	3.25	3.5	3.75	4.25	5	5.5	6	6.5	9.0

Annie's Attic®

TOLL-FREE ORDER LINE or to request a free catalog (800) LV-ANNIE (800) 582-6643
Customer Service (800) AT-ANNIE (800) 282-6643, **Fax** (800) 882-6643
Visit AnniesAttic.com
We have made every effort to ensure the accuracy and completeness of these instructions.
We cannot, however, be responsible for human error, typographical mistakes or variations in individual work.

ISBN: 978-1-59635-252-0